T0198701

Grit in the
Classroom

Grit in the Classroom

Building Perseverance for Excellence in Today's Students

Laila Y. Sanguras

Routledge
Taylor & Francis Group

NEW YORK AND LONDON

First published in 2017 by Prufrock Press Inc.

Published in 2021 by Routledge
605 Third Avenue, New York, NY 10017
2 Park Square, Milton Park, Abingdon, Oxon OX14 4RN

Routledge is an imprint of the Taylor & Francis Group, an informa business.

Library of Congress Cataloging-in-Publication Data

Names: Sanguras, Laila Y., 1977- author.
Title: Grit in the classroom : building perseverance for excellence in
  today's students / by Laila Y. Sanguras.
Description: Waco, Texas : Prufrock Press, Inc., [2017] | Includes
  bibliographical references.
Identifiers: LCCN 2017025482
Subjects: LCSH: Motivation in education. | Classroom environment.
Classification: LCC LB1065 .S26 2017 | DDC 370.15/4--dc23
LC record available at https://lccn.loc.gov/2017025482

ISBN-13: 978-1-0321-4276-0 (hbk)
ISBN-13: 978-1-6182-1631-1 (pbk)

DOI: 10.4324/9781003235385

Table of Contents

Acknowledgments

To begin, I need to thank every former student for being my inspiration and for teaching me how little I know. From that first day of school in Hood River, OR, to my last in Coppell, TX, I tried my very best with every one of you. I appreciate every time you challenged me to be better than I am. You, my wacky middle schoolers, fascinate me.

I also want to thank my children who have taught me so much about the importance of grit. What's more is that you now have proof that Mama wrote a book and at least one person bought a copy, so I've got some street cred now. I love you all more than more, Brycen, Hayden, Emma Kate, Anika, Beckam, and Cole.

I need to give a literary head nod to my editor, Katy, for being amazingly patient with me and for believing in this nontraditional, yet educational, book. Thank you for not thinking I'm crazy.

Finally, I want to thank my husband. From our brainstorming walks at the beginning to the celebratory toasts at the end, you've given me the belief I needed in myself that I could do this and the support I needed to get it done. Let's grab some books and hit the beach, babe.

Chapter 1
Anatomy of Grit

From pretty much my first day as a teacher in a small Oregon town, I started asking, why? Why won't they do their homework? Why don't they care about this stuff? Why can't I motivate them?

I never doubted why I was teaching or why I was there, but I just couldn't figure out why I struggled to engage some of my students. I tried everything I could think of, I experienced little to no success, and then I went to graduate school. I studied motivation at Portland State University in Portland, OR, and then went on to focus on coping, resiliency, and mental toughness at the University of North Texas in Denton, TX. And then, many years later, I was sitting in a staff meeting in a suburban Texas town and was shown Angela Duckworth's 2013 TED talk on grit.

In her talk, Duckworth (2013) described the challenges of teaching math to middle school kids. (No kidding, right?) She noticed that the students who performed the best in her class weren't necessarily the smartest—they were the ones who worked the hardest. As a graduate student at the University of Pennsylvania, Duckworth and her research team studied teachers, salespeople, and West Point cadets in order to learn more. Interestingly, they found that grit was the best predictor of success. Not IQ, prior achievement, or great hair . . . but grit.

DOI: 10.4324/9781003235385-1

The problem, according to Duckworth, was that educators have been too narrowly focused. Although we are really good at measuring achievement, she argued that we needed to consider how grit can be assessed and improved in our students if we really wanted to build their stamina and increase their likelihood for success in school and beyond.

I was completely inspired after watching Duckworth's talk. Her ideas made sense, which I appreciated as a teacher, and they were supported by research, which I valued as an educational psychologist. I wanted to do more, however, to inspire other teachers the way I was inspired during that staff meeting. So, here we are. I've outlined practical ideas for how teachers, parents, and administrators can work together to recognize and instill grit in their students.

This chapter provides a framework for the pages ahead. We're going to rewind to the 19th century in order to examine intelligence and how the conception of this construct has changed over time. We're also going to dissect grit so that we can study each component in depth. And that's only Chapter 1!

In Chapter 2, we're going to dig deeper into how grit is measured and examine ways teachers can support students in their grit development. Chapter 3 is focused on building grit in gifted students, specifically as it relates to elite talent development, and what all classrooms can learn from the field of gifted education. In Chapter 4, I integrate grit with what we know about growth mindset research and how teachers can use these theories in working with students. Because passion is such an integral component to grit, I've dedicated all of Chapter 5 to how teachers can cultivate passion in their students. I wrote Chapter 6 as a guide to help you work with parents, ensuring a streamlined approach to building grit in students. And finally, the last chapter is all about grit at the school level and how campus staff and administrators can work together to build a gritty school culture.

Each chapter ends with final thoughts and discussion questions to help you consider practical ways you can apply these ideas to your classrooms. I also included a compilation of resources at the end of the book that I hope is helpful to you. By the last page, if I've done my job well, you will be inspired and equipped with the knowledge you need to prioritize the building of grit in your students.

Intelligence Versus Grit

Beginning with Sir Francis Galton in the late 1800s, psychologists have been enamored by the individual differences that make up varying levels of intelligence. Studying intelligence began as a very practical matter: Educators needed to identify which students would need special help in school, and the military needed to quickly assess the abilities of its recruits. There were even some years when scientists toyed with the idea of limiting procreation to those who met certain intellectual criteria. I'm not kidding.

You are likely familiar with the Stanford-Binet Intelligence Scales, a five-factor instrument that assesses fluid reasoning, knowledge, quantitative reasoning, visual-spatial processing, and working memory (Roid, 2003). The scales have undergone five iterations since 1916 and are frequently used to determine appropriate special education interventions.

Most recently, Howard Gardner's (2000) theory of multiple intelligences started discussions centered on the myriad ways we can demonstrate intelligence. Gardner identified the following learning styles: visual-spatial, bodily-kinesthetic, musical, interpersonal, intrapersonal, linguistic, and logical-mathematical. His research inspired an explosion of ideas in the teaching world. Teachers tailored their instruction to the learning styles of their students, but even still, they continued to struggle with motivating their students and increasing their achievement.

Clearly, we don't have this intelligence thing figured out just yet. But who really cares? Intelligence does not guarantee success or happiness or world peace. High school reunions are full of smart people who accomplished little. Keeping up with old friends on social media reveals stories of people with limited intelligence who surprised everyone by their achievements. Sure, there is research to indicate that performance, particularly in traditional learning environments, can be predicted by intelligence. But we are finding that something more is needed in this society of hashtags, drones, and self-parking cars.

Grit is about internal fortitude and zeal.

That something else may be grit. Duckworth (2016), a professor and researcher, has become the name associated with grit. She defined *grit* as sustained perseverance coupled with intense passion. Notice the absence of *intelligence* in that definition. Furthermore, what else is missing? Luck, talent, wealth, fairy godmother. . . . According to Duckworth, people can be successful if they can persevere through challenges and if they are passionate about their pursuit. Of course, it's easier to pursue when one has luck, talent, wealth, or a fairy godmother, but grit isn't about easy. Grit is about internal fortitude and zeal. It requires commitment, thick skin, and (I'm sure you've already guessed it) self-discipline.

Self-Discipline

Self-discipline is the ability to control an impulse in order to overcome a weakness. It's the ability to not grab a handful of Skittles when you pass by the candy bowl, to stay in and study when you want to meet up with your friends, to not respond to a text message while driving. This control over your behavior is based on a value judgment; you are making a difficult decision to pick the "better" choice.

This obviously implies that you recognize which one is the better choice. Raise your hand if you've taught a student who struggles with impulse control, who has absolutely no concept that a "better" choice even exists. I know we've all been there. Although the ability to manage our impulses improves as we age, it's definitely related to maturity, temperament, and genetics (Dewar, 2011–2015; Smith, Mick, & Faraone, 2009). I'm sure you're thinking (again) that this is just one more thing you can't control about your students. And you're right.

Self-discipline is the ability to control an impulse in order to overcome a weakness.

However, there is an important part you play as a teacher. You can reward your students for exhibiting self-control. Depending on the age of your students, this could be the amount of time your students work independently or how they transition from activity to activity. The reward you provide could be a silly sticker, authentic and specific praise, or extra free time. The point is that you recognize and reinforce what you want to see in your students.

Wilhelm Hofmann and his colleagues (2013) studied self-control and how it relates to happiness. They found that people with higher self-control are not only happier with their lives, but happier in the moment they made the controlled choice. This shocked me, as I regularly wrestle my health conscience over my late-night snacks. I usually eat my carrots with a snarl, wishing I had picked the cookies. Even further, they reported that people with higher self-control put themselves into fewer positions where they would have to make a difficult choice. Basically, they are saying to not buy the cookies in the first place. (Ugh.)

The influence self-discipline has on student achievement is astounding. In a study of eighth-grade students, Duckworth and Seligman (2005) found that students with higher self-discipline outperformed the others on attendance, grades, standardized test scores, and admission to a magnet high school. Self-discipline explained more variance in these measures than IQ. See? I told you intelligence was nothing to fret over. Grittier people are also more likely to keep their jobs, graduate from high school, and stay married (Duckworth & Seligman, 2005). That's something, y'all.

And it's not even a research fad! We're talking Francis Galton in 1869, William James in 1890, and Sigmund Freud in 1920 *all* found that the ability to regulate one's behavior was crucial to success. And their findings have been replicated so many times since then (Caprara, Vecchione, Alessandri, Gerbino, & Barbaranelli, 2011; Tangney, Baumeister, & Boone, 2004; Zimmerman & Kitsantas, 2014). Self-discipline is important.

Duckworth (2016) proposed that goals are built into a hierarchy with actions at the bottom and goals above, all leading to a super stretch goal. Grit is the ability to stay focused on that super goal, regardless of distractions and setbacks. Self-control is the ability to choose to complete the actions leading to that goal instead of choosing an activity that does not lead to the goal. It doesn't necessarily even need to be a negative activity. For example, my super goal was to write a bestselling book about grit in the classroom that would be so revered that I would end up on a float in the Macy's Thanksgiving Day Parade. (Yes, I realize there are some issues with my logic here, but a girl can dream.) A lower goal was to read Angela Duckworth's (2016) book on grit. An activity leading to that goal was reading every day. A competing activity was picking up a "fun" book to read (sorry, Angela). Reading the "fun" book isn't going to harm me, but it's also not getting me any closer to my super goal. Encouraging students to attain their goals can be accomplished in much the same way. Figure 1 is an example of a student's super goal. Attaining a super goal requires self-discipline, which ultimately leads to perseverance.

Perseverance

Perseverance is a behavior, a purposeful action to pursue a goal or task despite obstacles. Perseverance is Kennedy Cobble,

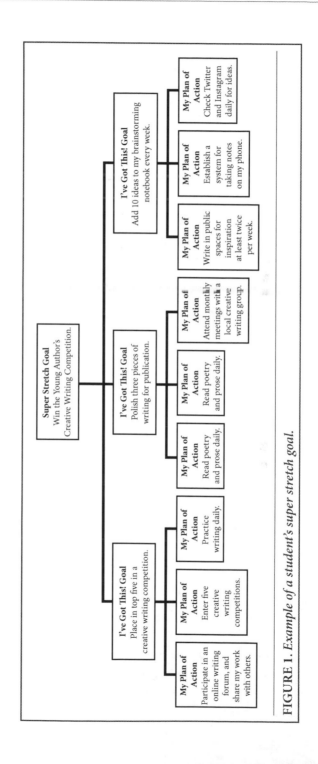

FIGURE 1. *Example of a student's super stretch goal.*

who started her battle with cancer a decade ago at 14. Since then, she's beat cancer four times and is now pursuing a career in education (Minutaglio, 2016). Perseverance is Jack Andraka who was rejected 199 times before he was granted a science lab at Johns Hopkins University to develop an easy and inexpensive test to detect pancreatic cancer (Tucker, 2012). Perseverance is Mustafa Khaleefah, who moved to the United States as an Iraqi refugee in sixth grade, started playing football as a high school sophomore, was heavily recruited by a dozen colleges, and then committed to Michigan State University (McCabe, 2016).

I encourage you to brainstorm this idea of perseverance as it applies to people you and your students know. The reason why this is important is simple: It's easy to talk about the perseverance of these unique individuals, but many of us don't have Kennedy's experiences (thankfully), Jack's opportunities, or Mustafa's circumstances. It's not easy to recognize perseverance in ourselves and in the people we know. And if we can't recognize it, how can we celebrate and repeat it?

Perseverance is a behavior, a purposeful action to pursue a goal or task despite obstacles.

Perseverance is *not* to be confused with compliance. One way to think of compliance is the adherence to rules and expectations. Anyone who has participated in a school fire drill knows that compliance is important here. However, another kind of compliance is the submissive, unengaged completion of assigned tasks. This type of compliance should in no way be the goal of a teacher. If you're a sheep herder or a snake charmer? Fine. But not a teacher. The difference lies in where the behavior begins. Compliance is something forced onto you. It's like saying you're sorry just to end an argument, even when you don't feel sorry. You're not committed enough to approach the conflict with an attitude of perseverance. You would rather just give in and move on. (I may be speaking from experience here.) Classrooms are full of students completing assignments out of compliance. They're quiet and working, but far from engaged. When faced with a challenge, their effort will be minimal toward solving it—if they don't just give up. Students who complete their assignments out of compliance are not going to become gritty. They aren't developing a passion, and they won't persevere when things get tough.

In a 2016 *Fortune* 500 Insiders Network forum, Greg Hyslop, the chief technology officer of The Boeing Company, made the case that perseverance is the most important skill a millennial can have. Hyslop argued that most of Boeing's projects could take a decade or more to complete, but that many younger employees won't stick around to their completion. Those who stay with a project long term learn the problem solving and conflict management skills that are critical to being successful in innovative fields. Those who quit and move onto the next shiny object miss out on those skills. (Go ahead and picture one of those people right now. I know you know one.)

Showing perseverance, especially in an imperfect situation, shows that you are trustworthy. In the wise words of Tom Petty and the Heartbreakers, "You can stand me up at the gates of hell, but I won't back down." Obviously the particular gates of hell can vary throughout your life—the point is you don't give up. By sticking with something, you show those around you that you are committed to the task, regardless of the obstacle.

Additionally, by not giving up, you are also teaching yourself some valuable lessons. You recognize that your life is in your control, that you dictate what happens. In this realization, you gain power over the decisions you make. You can also learn something from the pursuit of a challenge, perhaps expanding your interests in a new direction. Imagine what this can do for your students, your students who are shuffled from class to class, who have little say in their daily activities or routines. But they do have control over how they respond to the obstacles they experience, and, in that moment, they have the power needed to build grit.

Perseverance often shows up in schools via character education. (Groan.) A well-meaning teacher leads a class discussion about Albert Einstein, Vincent van Gogh, or Dr. Seuss, asking her class to imagine what would have happened if those icons of creativity had given up. Another teacher turns a lively debate away from whether Haymitch is a hero or villain in *The Hunger Games* into a lesson on the determination one needs to fight oppression. All of a sudden, she's squelching her students' excitement in order to teach a "life lesson." But perseverance can't be taught in an isolated lesson. It's personal, and it's complicated.

Grit involves *sustained* perseverance.

In the 1930s, the administrators at Lenox School, a boys' preparatory school in Massachusetts, were searching for a method to test applicants' level of perseverance. They relied on intelligence testing to screen the boys, but also wanted to measure this trait that they felt was equally important when preparing for college. So, Walter Clark (1935) developed two tests where students were asked to create words from a given set of letters and to do something similar with numbers. Clark (1935) also asked the instructors to rate the boys' perseverance in class and when completing their extracurricular activities. He found that the word and number tests were fairly reliable in measuring perseverance. The test administrators acknowledged that a limitation of their study was that they could not control for the motivation of the boys; they were simply relying on them to try their best because they asked them to.

This motivation is key. Remember that grit involves *sustained* perseverance. So, although Clark's (1935) tests for perseverance may have initially detected a certain level of "stick-to-itiveness," they likely didn't reveal information the administrators found useful. However, in addition to overcoming some pretty extreme obstacles, Kennedy, Jack, and Mustafa (discussed at the beginning of this section) were also highly motivated and passionate about their pursuits. If they were ambivalent about their goals, they likely wouldn't continue pursuing them. This is where passion comes in. Perseverance is often confused with grit, but grit *only* exists when sustained perseverance is paired with passion.

Passion

Common sense tells us about the importance of passion in our enjoyment of something. The more you enjoy it, the more likely you are to put in the practice needed to be successful. It's extremely difficult to excel at something you don't like and gives you no pleasure. For example, I will never be the lima-bean-eating champion of West Cape May, NJ (Alexander, 1988). Why? I don't like lima beans. I have zero interest in eating one lima, let alone the 600 it takes to win the contest. I don't want to wear the "World's Largest Source of Natural Gas" shirt as a prize. There is nothing in it for me, and there is no amount of information you can tell me about the greatness of limas to change my mind. No interest equals no passion. But what about someone who does like lima beans? How do we take a sincere interest and develop it into a passion? And how do we do that in school?

Grit *only* exists when sustained perseverance is paired with passion.

The key may be to explore "passion for learning" (PFL), not just passion. PFL is sustained and focused interest that captivates a child's time. Other activities are likely discarded because they take time away from this specific interest. Additionally, the presence of PFL in a child may predict the presence of passion as an adult. In their 2013 study of PFL in children, Larry Coleman and Aige Guo examined children who sustained PFL on a specific domain for at least 12 months. They described six middle school students who exhibited PFL in a variety of domains; three were homeschooled and three were not. To give you an example of what PFL looks like, I want to describe Billy to you:

> Billy's PFL was preaching. His parents told the researchers that Billy was uninterested in typical children's toys and that he loved to sing songs he heard in church at a very young age. His goal was to read the King James Bible before kindergarten and he had a congregation by the age of 13. Billy tried traditional school, but was frequently in trouble for anointing the other students with water or oil. He refused to participate in activities that went against his religion and would only wear a bishop's attire (i.e., black suit, black shoes, and gold cross). And that was in kindergarten. . . . Billy described his schoolwork as a middle schooler as detestable and displayed excitement when explaining how he counseled and shared God's word with his congregation. (Coleman & Guo, 2013 p. 12).

Coleman and Guo (2013) also interviewed Betty, a passionate speller.

> Like Billy, Betty's interest began prior to kindergarten and she also passed on outside activities to stay focused on pursuing her passion. However, even though Betty's interest was much less controversial than Billy's, she described cultivating her passion for spelling *in spite of* the confines of school. She dedicated 40 hours a week to studying, fitting it in when she could: on the bus, between classes, and during downtime. She never mentioned being given time to study during school. (p. 13)

Should time in school be dedicated to pursuing passions?

Dr. Joseph Renzulli thinks so. Renzulli is an educational psychologist who has worked in gifted education for decades. In my house, he's been dubbed the Godfather of the Gifted because of his contribution and commitment to gifted education. (I call him G.G. Kidding. Okay, just not to his face.) He developed a three-part Venn diagram of giftedness, called the Three-Ring Conception of Giftedness (see Figure 2), that defines gifted behaviors as some combination of above-average ability, task commitment, and creativity (Renzulli, 1984). Task commitment has also been described as sustained perseverance. An implication of this model is that the amount one has in any area can change over time, but that the presence of all three indicate a level of giftedness that may not be supported in a traditional learning environment.

So, Renzulli (1984) developed the Enrichment Triad Model (see Figure 3), a three-pronged approach to meeting the needs of gifted students. It has since evolved into a model used to enrich the learning experiences of children of varying abilities. Type I Enrichment includes general exploratory activities to inspire students and expose them to an array of disciplines and interests. Type II Enrichment is focused on developing the critical thinking and problem-solving skills necessary when cultivating interest and creativity. Although Type I activities can be structured, Type II are more organic, stemming from students' needs. Type III Enrichment is similar to developing one's passion for learning. Students who are committed to their interests immerse themselves in them and are "creatively engaged" in this process.

Robert Vallerand and his colleagues (2003) have studied passion for more than a decade. They define passion as a strong desire for an activity, object, or person that one loves, values, and invests time and energy into. In their dualistic model of passion, two types of passion exist: harmonious and obsessive.

If you have harmonious passion for an activity, you do it because you get joy from it. You are intrinsically motivated to engage in the activity and this passion does not interfere with other parts of your life. For example, if, like me, you feel harmonious passion toward young adult literature, you are rarely happier

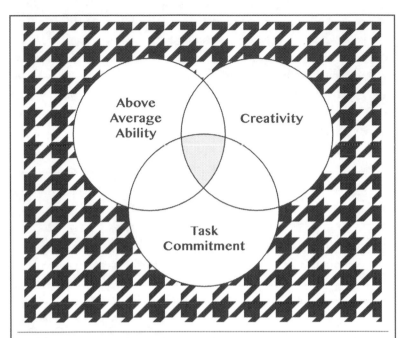

FIGURE 2. *Three-Ring Conception of Giftedness. N te. F om* The Schoolwide Enrichment Model: A How-to Guide for T alent Development *(3rd ed., p. 22), by J. S. Renzulli and S. M. Reis, 2014, Waco, TX: Taylor & Francis Group Copyright 2014 by Taylor & Francis Group Reprinted with permission.*

than when curled up with the newest John Green gem. If you had a choice of what to do in your free time, you would likely choose reading. You're also inclined to make recommendations to friends and experience pure joy when you meet someone with this same passion. Harmonious passion is typically viewed as a positive behavior and is internalized as a healthy part of your identity.

> Passion is a strong desire for an activity, object, or person that one loves, values, and invests time and energy into (Vallerand et al., 2003).

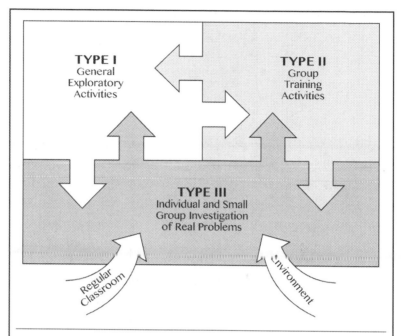

FIGURE 3. *The Enrichment Triad Model. Note. From* The Schoolwide Enrichment Model: A How-to Guide for Talent Development *(3rd ed., p. 50), by J. S. Renzulli and S. M. Reis, 2014, Waco, TX: Taylor & Francis Group.Copyright 2014 by Taylor & Francis Group. Reprinted with permission.*

If you have obsessive passion for an activity, your behavior is more maladaptive and can lead to conflict. Your passion supersedes everything else to the point where you will risk relationships, work, and other important parts of your life in order to cater to your interest. If you can't imagine this really being a thing, pop by my house when a certain college football team is playing and tell my husband you want to take him to his favorite place in the world for dinner. You'll likely be eating alone. Obsessive passion is similar to an addiction, where the excitement for an activity, object, or person is so extreme that the person is blind to most everything else. It's also internalized as a consuming part of your identity; without this passion, you don't know who you are or what to care about.

We see similar obsessive passion in our students when we try to transition them from an activity they don't want to stop, or in our children when we limit their screen time. It may not be that these activities are part of their identity—it's just that their interest is more powerful than anything you're offering.

Although persistent pursuit of passion is integral to establishing grit, flexibility is also important. One must be able to distinguish between harmonious and obsessive behavior, adapting to new situations in a healthy manner. For example, my husband has realized over time that he is terrible company when he tries to combine his passion with any other activity; while obsessive at times, his self-awareness minimizes the potential for conflict.

Interestingly, the amount of time you spend on a task does not determine whether your passion is harmonious or obsessive. The key is how you feel about what you are doing. If you feel in control of your time and emotions while pursuing your passion, it is likely more harmonious than obsessive. If you are feeling like you must commit to your passion or you will think poorly of yourself, or feel that others will think badly of you, it's likely that your passion is unhealthy. Because a person with obsessive passion builds her identity around the passion, how well she is accomplishing her goals in relation to the passion impacts how she feels about herself. Pursuing the passion becomes more rigid and less creative, as there is little room for failure.

Grit in School

Most of us entered the field of education because we want to make a difference in children's lives. We believe in education, and we believe that teachers are a crucial component of a child's educational experience. There is nothing worse than feeling like you failed a child, that no matter what you tried or what your intentions were, you didn't make the difference you aspired to. Sure, you can tell yourself that maybe you just can't see that influence until later in life. But if we step out of fantasyland for a moment, we will face reality: There are some kids we won't reach. There are some kids we fail. And for that, we're deeply sorry and regretful. We're also committed to figuring out what *else* we can do. Because we believe in the power of education, we believe that there is something to learn from these dark moments. And that's why we study and read. That's why you're here.

Grit may have just as important an influence on success as cognitive ability.

Let's come back to cognitive ability for a moment. Duckworth (2016) argued that grit may be a significant predictor of success, possibly more of a predictor than cognitive ability. In 1904, Charles Spearman published a paper about a general factor of intelligence; he called this g. After studying the results of multiple batteries of achievement tests (i.e., visual, spatial, verbal, memory, etc.), he realized that scores were pretty similar across tests. That is, a person who earned a low score on one test, earned similarly low scores on all tests. Additionally, researchers have repeatedly reported a strong positive relationship between g and IQ (Carroll, 1997; Gottfredson, 1998; Jenson, 1980; Spearman, 1904) For example, a person with a high g likely has a high IQ. Why should you care? Because g, and therefore IQ, is fairly stable over time. Assuming you take a reliable IQ test as an adolescent, the percentile rank of your IQ will be similar when you take another test as an older adult. Now you're probably thinking this is a big downer. I mean, if we can't increase intelligence, why do we get up every morning and put on our teacher pants? Well, because according to Duckworth and her colleagues (Duckworth, Peterson, Matthews, & Kelly, 2007), grit may have just as important an influence on success as cognitive ability. Mic drop.

Walk through this with me. You're an average student who decides to take an advanced placement (AP) course your junior year of high school. You need the college credit and want to prove you can do this. You study, meet with your teacher during tutoring hours, and complete all of your assignments. You struggle here and there, but ultimately earn a high grade in the class and score a 3 on the test. You worked your way through this course and earned college credit as a junior. Your intelligence hasn't changed. But you know more than you did when you started. You have improved study habits. You believe in yourself and what you are capable of. That's grit.

Have you ever popped into a school and overheard two teachers bragging to one another about the IQs of their students? Nope. What do we care about in education? Because I don't know you and I'm not going to make any assumptions, I'll tell you what we should care about—the 10 things listed in Table 1.

To be clear, these are not cultivated through character education or weekly role-playing. We must design learning experiences that thrust children into practicing these behaviors over and over and over again. Think of the entire school year as one big project-based learning adventure. We don't design a lesson that is going to require students to complete a service-learning project in order to demonstrate empathy; we are going to design rigorous history lessons that require students to view events from multiple perspectives. We won't force a student to work on a science project for a month; we will create a challenging lesson that leads students to ask unlimited questions and give them time to find the answers.

Grit will not solve all of our problems. After all, we are dealing with people and people are unpredictable. However, grit is something we can grasp onto as one tool to improve how we approach education.

So, although you may not hear teachers bragging about a student's IQ, it's common to hear discussions of talent. Duckworth suggested that by explaining achievement (or lack of) by way of talent, we are being lazy (as cited in Lebowitz, 2016a). We are attributing something great (i.e., success) to something we just innately have, something we're born with. So, we can either wish on a star or we can dig deeper.

TABLE 1

10 Things We Should Care About in Education

1.	Children believe they can learn and they demonstrate growth in their learning over time.
2.	Children love the process of discovery so much that they lose track of time.
3.	Children know how to approach a challenge and problem solve their way through it.
4.	Children feel empathy and genuine respect for others.
5.	Children are passionate and can articulate their passions.
6.	Children understand that they control their actions and, therefore, the results of those actions.
7.	Children know what it feels like to want to give up—but then they persevere through it.
8.	Children establish the necessary self-discipline to achieve short- and long-term goals.
9.	Children are intrinsically motivated because of their dedication to the learning process.
10.	Children understand their strengths and weaknesses and that these are not fixed.

Introducing Students to Grit

By now you realize that grit isn't something that your students will just learn through a flashy activity. It's a skill that needs to be nurtured over time. There are, however, steps you can take to put grit at the forefront of your students' minds. After all, it's much easier to develop a skill if you're equipped with the understanding of what that skill looks like.

You can assist students in constructing an understanding of grit by introducing them to people who have demonstrated passion and perseverance in pursuit of their goals. Depending on the abilities of your students, choose the reading selections accordingly.

Students can read biographies of J. K. Rowling or Angie Thomas in language arts, Marie Curie or Albert Einstein in science, Nelson Mandela or Abraham Lincoln in social studies, and Isaac Newton and Marjorie Lee Browne in mathematics. Of course, you could also select a number of other people including Michael Jordan, Frida Kahlo, and Jay Z. Most people who have "made it" in their fields have done so because of grit. By providing students with biographies of these individuals, this is the conclusion your students should reach.

Never miss a moment to bring grit to the forefront of your students' minds.

It's also fun to introduce concepts to students using television and movies. I've found that you can't go wrong with Disney, whether your students are 8 or 18. The main characters in TV shows such as *Austin & Ally*, *Jessie*, and *Shake It Up* all demonstrate passion and perseverance. And who can argue the grit of Ariel in *The Little Mermaid*? Or Pinocchio? You can show a short clip to your students and ask them to identify the actions that demonstrate grit. You can also ask students to identify areas of weakness—where characters could have made different decisions to attain their goals.

Of course, it's most important that students recognize grit in themselves and those around them. Ask them to journal about someone they know personally who exemplifies (or doesn't) the kind of passion and perseverance needed to be successful. When discussing current or historical events with your students, make sure "grit" is part of the conversation. Never miss a moment to bring grit to the forefront of your students' minds.

When students understand what grit is all about, you can show them Table 2. This table is a list of ways in which students may demonstrate grit and warning signs that they may not be demonstrating grit. Ask students to add specific behaviors and

TABLE 2

Student Demonstrations of Grit or Lack of Grit

Signs of Students Demonstrating Grittiness	Warning Signs of Students Without Grit
• They get a bad grade on a math test and ask you how they can do better next time. • You introduce a project, and your students get excited about the possibilities. • They can be overly chatty in group projects but typically related to the assignment.	• They get huffy when they get a bad grade, throwing away their tests. • They are annoyed by the open-endedness of a project and just want you to tell them how to get a good grade. • They ask you for extra credit, often at the end of the grading period.

actions to the table so that they can apply what they've learned. It's imperative to be explicit in what grit does and does not look like so they can begin to transfer their understanding to their own experiences.

Pursuing Excellence

Duckworth and Gross (2014) proposed two equations to explain how talent leads to achievement (p. 44).

Talent × Effort = Skill
Skill × Effort = Achievement

Notice that effort counts in both equations. In fact, if I'm remembering my high school algebra correctly, you can rewrite the equations as

$$(\text{Talent} \times \text{Effort}) \times \text{Effort} = \text{Achievement}$$
or
$$\text{Talent} \times \text{Effort}^2 = \text{Achievement}$$

Okay, I know I'm just showing off now, but you should really just pause to consider the power of this path to achievement. Sure, talent is important, but effort is even *more* influential. That's pretty awesome.

Several years ago I had the opportunity to work with three elite gymnasts. They had been "gym-schooled" through eighth grade while they trained 40+ hours in the gym. One of them lived with a host family during the week so she could train and then went home on the weekends to see her parents and brother. The gymnasts' days started early and ended late. I was fortunate enough to be their freshman English teacher. I created a blended course for them; I worked with them in person 3 days a week and they worked at home or the gym the other days.

It is crucial that we help our students find their "why."

These girls were extremely talented and had been selected to train with Olympic champion Kim Zmeskal Burdette in her Texas gym. Their skill (talent x effort) was undeniable. Duckworth (2016) argued that something happens between skill and achievement. In a sense, having a skill is easy: You have a talent and you put in the effort to develop that talent. However, to take that skill and to turn it into achievement, you have to put forth even *more* effort. For my gymnasts to compete internationally, earn college scholarships, and have a chance at the Olympics, they had to stay committed. They had to persevere through every challenge presented to them in and out of the gym in order to achieve their goals. The "why" behind the commitment for these girls was their passion.

Although they didn't love every drill and every injury, they loved the competition and the pursuit of excellence.

In school, it is crucial that we help our students find their "why." If you don't think we need to figure out how to do this, ask a kid in the back of the classroom why he needs to be in your class. It's very likely the answers will range from "I don't know" to "because I have to." He has no "why," and, after his response, you may also be wondering why you even need to be there.

If you're like me (a mostly left-brainer who occasionally dips her toe in the right-brain world), you get very excited when you use algebra in real life, because, despite the posters listing *all* of the careers that use math, you really don't care. However, when I am trying to figure out how much the to-die-for Vince Camuto pumps will be after the discount, I visualize the equation in my head, do the math on my smartphone, and mentally thank my algebra teacher. (I also start plotting a way to bring these gorgeous shoes home without anyone noticing.) But, you want to know something? I still don't care about math. I do care about getting a good deal, and fashion is definitely one of my passions, so that's my "why." It's personal.

But, listen. I am not advocating that math teachers create problems around students' interests. My algebra teacher could have forced me to calculate the sale prices of a thousand pairs of shoes and I still wouldn't care about math. Solving equations has nothing to do with my passions now or as a high school student. So what was the point of taking that class? Well, in addition to it being required (the kid in the back of the room was right), I learned to respect the discipline. I appreciated how every variable had a place in an equation and I learned that if I took my time, I could solve multistep problems correctly. I also learned that, because math didn't come easily to me, I had to put in extra time to learn the material. And, most importantly, I learned that when I did learn something difficult, I felt a great amount of pride (#perseverance).

With these equations, Duckworth (2016) suggested that some-one twice as talented who puts forth half the effort as another person may have the same level of skill as that person, but will achieve less over time. Read that sentence again. Draw it out if you have to. Crunch the numbers. As a teacher, this is the greatest thing I've heard since SSR (silent sustained reading) made a comeback. When we place an emphasis on effort, authentic effort, with our students, we are also showing them a way to improve their performance. And by creating a community that values true effort, you are creating individuals who know how to take their skills, pursue their passions, and excel.

Sam was a student I failed. I completely thought I had him figured out; he was an extremely bright, underperforming student in seventh grade, but I was going to turn him around. So, in my eighth-grade language arts class, I reserved one day a week for independent study. I gave very few guidelines regarding the topics students could choose and set up research checkpoints. Students informally reported to the class their findings, as a way to generate more interest and expose one another to a variety of topics. I mean, I was teacher of the year material here.

> When we place an emphasis on effort,
> authentic effort, with our students,
> we are also showing them a way to
> improve their performance.

Sam chose to research the dark web, the underworld of the world wide web. His first informal presentation was fascinating. His second presentation . . . not so much. He repeated almost the exact same information to the class. I was going to quietly pull him aside later to discuss the fact that he had done *nothing* this past month (remember, I'm teacher of the year material), but Julia said what we all were thinking: "Isn't this the same thing you told us last month?" Sam's response: "There is no other information available on this topic. It's all classified." Okey-doke. Sam clearly had the skill to knock our socks off with his research, but he didn't have the effort. Maybe his interest in the topic was weak. Maybe he didn't have enough self-discipline to sustain his focus. Maybe he was tired. I don't know, but that's okay. Because learning and passion are so personal, I am incapable of having all of the answers. We have to let ourselves off the hook and just enjoy the challenge. For many of us, that challenge is our passion. Am I right?

On the other hand, Jorge was more successful. He was not a naturally talented student and struggled to keep up with all of his assignments. His research topic and questions were very simplistic; let me tell you, this boy really loved penguins. He had to put in a tremendous amount of effort for every part of his study, from citing sources to writing up his results coherently. By the end of the semester, however, his research questions evolved to include bigger issues about penguins in captivity and the effects global warming were having on their livelihood. Jorge demonstrated grit, while also learning research skills, to believe in himself, and critical thinking skills. Go ahead and say it: #teacheroftheyear.

Final Thoughts

Be a yardstick of quality. Some people aren't used to an environment where excellence is expected.

—Steve Jobs

Grit is the result of intense passion coupled with sustained perseverance and it may be the difference between success and failure over time. In building grit, effort counts twice—more than achievement and more than talent. As teachers who give our students everything we have (and then some), we can take practical steps to cultivate grit in our students.

Self-discipline and passion are also important to our understanding of grit. School is the place where we can help our students manage their behaviors and stoke their passions. As teachers, we can fulfill the dual purposes of teaching our students content while developing their abilities to persevere through challenges.

Discussion Questions

1. Describe a time you faced a challenge and persevered. How did you feel before, during, and after? What about a time that you gave up or were defeated?
2. Read over the "10 Things We Should Care About in Education" (p. 19). Do any of these not belong? Is anything missing?
3. Review Duckworth's equations for grit (p. 22). Do you agree? Can you think of an example when effort influenced achievement more than talent?

Chapter 2

Measuring Grit

Grit is "doing what you love, but not just falling in love— *staying* in love." (Duckworth, 2016, p. 54)

When I started my doctoral program at the University of North Texas, I picked the most difficult concentration I could find within the field of education and applied for that program (#nojoke). I felt I had gone through many years of schooling with minimal challenges and that if I were going to pursue a Ph.D., I wanted to feel the sense of accomplishment that follows a challenge. I selected research, measurement, and statistics as my concentration and dove right in. It was incredibly difficult and scary (I still shudder when I hear the word "matrix"), but I persevered. Not only that, but I have a great respect for measurement theory and how instruments can inform teaching practices. In this chapter, we're going to explore the measurement of grit and discuss what this means for you.

Duckworth and her colleagues could not find an instrument to appropriately measure grit, so they developed the Grit Scale. In her book, Duckworth (2016) published a 10-item Grit Scale (p. 55); she also provides links to 8- and 12-item Grit Scales on her website (https://angeladuckworth.com/research). The results are used to calculate a "grittiness" score. It's important to note that

DOI: 10.4324/9781003235385-2

grittiness can change. Depending on the tasks ahead of you, you may be feeling very committed and focused at one time and then ready to move on to something more interesting another time. Additionally, like the development of the frontal lobe, grit develops as one ages. We can see that in the attention spans of children; as they age, they are more capable of focusing for longer periods of time.

Interestingly, the items that measure passion don't really ask about the emotions we think of related to passion: excitement, fascination, craving. Instead, the items refer to being distracted by new ideas and maintaining focus. That's because, Duckworth (2016) argued, it's easy to be enthusiastic about something, but sustaining that enthusiasm is the hard part. My garage is full of sporting equipment that my kids never use anymore. My son would come home from camp or a friend's house beyond excited about a new sport, so we would get him some equipment and put him on a team. He would never complain about going to practice and would give everything he had in every game, but I could always tell that this "passion" wasn't going to last. When he wasn't at practice or a game, he chose to ride his bike, play video games, or play another sport altogether. Although he enjoyed the sport, he wasn't passionate about it—which is fine, by the way. He's only 9 years old. He just hasn't found his "thing" yet.

> ## If our students don't have interests that develop into passions, then they just haven't found the right one.

J. K. Rowling said, "If you don't like to read, you haven't found the right book." As a language arts teacher, this quote resonated with me as I accepted the mission of finding *the* book for each of my students. The same is true of finding interests. If our students don't have interests that develop into passions, then they just haven't found the right one. So we have this awesome opportunity to spark their interests and fan the flames. Not only do we get to see the excited glimmers in their eyes, but we are also building their capacity to maintain their enthusiasm for an interest over time.

It's interesting to view the perseverance items as a separate group. This half of the scale includes words like "setbacks" and "hard worker" (Duckworth, 2016, p. 55). I bet most people would use these words when defining "grit" without realizing the passion is missing. Perseverance is when you're running a marathon and don't think you can take another step, but you do. It's when you're working on your dissertation and have come to despise your topic so much that you just can't keep writing, but you do. It's about maintaining focus on something, despite the challenges along the way, but it certainly doesn't mean you are passionate about it. And without passion, there is no grit.

I am not advocating that you repeatedly administer the Grit Scale to your students. For one, it's a self-report measure, so they can answer however they want. Your answers are as reliable as the kids taking the instrument. It would take my eighth graders .07 seconds to decide to answer randomly or deliberately to try to earn a certain score. It's not like I'm going to yell at sweet Jenny, "Your interests *don't* change from year to year, now change your response!" if I suspect she is trying to mess with me. But more importantly, it doesn't matter how they score. All that matters is that they (and you) are aware of what it takes to be gritty and design your learning experiences intentionally to build grit. So let's get on with it.

The Grit Scale is useful in our pursuit to build grit in our students. The items are written simply and are a tangible way for teachers to discuss the construct with students. Rather than pulling up a multitude of slides covering the components of grit, imagine discussing each item one at a time. Choose the items that you think will be most applicable to your students. It's not so important that you discuss all of the items on the 8, 10, or 12 item scale; what's important is that you capture the two sides of grit: passion and perseverance.

Ask students to rate themselves on an item at a time and then brainstorm ways that they could increase their scores. Have them consider their grittiness in a variety of contexts. Is their score higher in one class than in another? Or in soccer or band practice? These are important conversations to have if we really want to understand and build grit in our students.

Building Grit

In 1985, Dr. Benjamin Bloom outlined three stages of developing talent in children. The first stage is all about having fun, romancing the discipline, and receiving external rewards. These rewards, things like stickers and praise, come from teachers and parents and serve as encouragement to continue the pursuit of this interest. Interests at this stage can be broad or specific and change often.

In the second stage, this interest becomes a part of the child's identity. She starts to describe herself as a soccer player or writer and finds intrinsic motivation for digging deeper into the discipline. Teachers continue to emphasize the fun and excitement in learning, while also having high expectations. Parents support their child by finding appropriate classes, tutors, coaches, etc.

In the final stage, children find the larger meaning in their interests and work toward mastery. They love competition and enjoy the demands placed upon them. In finding a greater purpose, they identify careers that align with their interests. Teachers become mentors and share a similar passion and commitment for the discipline. Parents support their children's pursuits and continue to find (and fund) outside support.

Angela Duckworth (2016) identified four components of grit that support Bloom's (1985) theory:

- interest (early years, Bloom's Stage 1),
- practice (middle years, Bloom's Stage 2),

- purpose (Bloom's Stage 3), and
- hope.

By understanding each of these, we can deconstruct what it means to build grit.

Building Interest

Interest is at the heart of passion. Duckworth (2016) described this interest as having a childlike curiosity, a fascination that takes priority. It's the feeling of being in your element, the fire in your belly. I feel it when I walk into a bookstore or am giving a talk to teachers. It's not a feeling of accomplishment, it's a feeling of excitement for what's to come.

Most of the time, interest doesn't just arrive like a flash of lightning or a pizza delivery. The interest that leads to passion is often the result of trying lots of different things. Part of the childlike discovery is finding out what you enjoy and where your talents lie. It doesn't matter if it's a lasting passion or meaningful or fruitful. For example, I've always loved reading. At an early age, I would set my alarm clock early so that I could read before school. I don't go anywhere without a book and always have one downloaded on my phone in case I'll stand out too much with a hardback. But I've also had moments when I thought I wanted to be a fashion designer, a judge, and the President of the United States. Even though those interests didn't take me anywhere in my career, I still love fashion and am fascinated by the law and politics.

Passion Begins With Discovery

Ainissa Ramirez (2013) advocates for passion-based learning. Yes, this is a thing. As if we needed another PBL acronym . . . but it's a good one! She says that passion is at the heart of every PBL (and other) acronym we have in education. And she's right. The bottom line is that we need to engage our students in our content, and we do this by being actively passionate about it.

I'm a pretty shy person and don't care much for small talk or meeting new people (because then I'll have to engage in small talk). But, if I know I get to show up somewhere and talk about curriculum or engaging teaching strategies (or grit) I'm totally in. I was the same way in my classroom. I taught "The Raven" almost every year and every single year I was captivated by Edgar Allan Poe's mastery of language. I would always find something new in his rhythm or diction and then my mind was blown—right in front of my students. Now that's powerful stuff. When your students see you amazed by your discipline, that passion is contagious. They want to be the next ones to blow your mind or to find something interesting in Poe's work. It changes from a lesson on poetry to a scavenger hunt for awesomeness. Is your content not mind blowing? Remember that passion, especially when you reach expert levels of understanding, is more about the nuance. So read more, study more. Fascinate yourself so you can fascinate your students.

The tricky part of this is that it's not easy to blow your own mind, let alone someone else's. Welcome to teaching, right? We, as an educational system, have a problem with breadth and depth. Teaching broadly is an expectation so that we can cover the standards mandated for us by state organizations. However, without depth, we won't get anywhere near fascination. So what do we do? Well, we're teachers, so we do it all (#seriously).

Jal Mehta (2015) suggested that we design T-shaped curriculum. Essentially, the top part of the T symbolizes the breadth while the tail represents the depth. The breadth is where we add the bells and whistles—we use music, video clips, and interactive activities to engage our students and get them to take a bite out of what we're offering. This is when we really sell our content like a well-intentioned mountebank. It's surely fun, but isn't going to build fascination. It's akin to flying over a city—you may ooh and ah a couple of times, but you don't know enough to know what you want to know more of.

The depth is when you "buzz the tower" with a fly-by. You get close enough to incite interest so that students begin generating questions about the content. We know that interest is personal, so we allow students to choose the towers they want to buzz. Worst case, teachers choose the areas for students to deepen their learning. The crucial part is to pay attention to the sparks so that they can be fanned later.

> We need to engage our students in
> our content and we do this by being
> actively passionate about it.

In elementary and middle school, passion begins with discovery. Duckworth (2016) suggested that children need to be exposed to "interest-stimulating experiences." Think about this in the context of your school and classroom. How many times are students' interests triggered in a calculated way?

To begin, have students consider what they think about when their mind wanders. What do they care about and what do they find, like Billy in Chapter 1, "detestable?" Actually give students the task of making a note of when their minds wander and where they go when they leave us. That's some serious metacognition and is really insightful into their interests.

Promoting Curiosity

We also have to build our students' curiosity. The science teacher across the hall from me would tell his students, "People who are bored are boring people," when they would complain of boredom. He was so right. On his blog, Eric Barker (2016) explained our society's current situation perfectly: We are so used to reacting to stimuli (i.e., texts, snaps, tweets, etc.) that we don't know what to do when our brains are at rest. We confuse that rest with boredom and become passive, just waiting for the next technological prompt so that we can wake up and live.

As their language arts teacher, I would help my students with their write-ups for science fair. In talking to them about their topics, I was regularly perplexed by their apathy. One student would tell me he was testing to see which brand of soda maintained its fizz the longest. Another student was trying to determine how much water waterproof mascara could resist before it ran. I was so curious about where these ideas came from, and they would just shrug and say they couldn't think of anything else. And then a whole bunch of students simply had no clue what to study. *Really? How is this possible?*, I thought. They had a golden opportunity to answer a question they were wondering about and they were wasting it! I figured out that two things were happening here.

One, a typical science fair is no fun. We take something that gets at the heart of passion and interest and then we teach all of the joy out of it. What about a science fair where you don't have to make a trifold poster board to display your results? (Because, really, the construction of this exhibit does nothing to deepen understanding and is often a visual representation of the kids with overly hands-on parents juxtaposed against parents like me. My poor kids.) Yes, writing up results is important and there is a time and place for that. And regardless of interest, there are always going to be things we just have to do; however, we will only do those things if we are getting something valuable from it. In this case, a kid will write up his report if that means he gets to share his findings that he's super excited about. But if we are tied so tightly to this idea of writing the report that kids hate what they're doing, then we are going about this the wrong way.

Building interest is not something that can be done in isolation. Exposure to ideas breeds new ideas.

What about a science fair where the only display is one sentence, a well-crafted cliffhanger that begs people to ask questions? Something like: *Maybelline causes brokenhearted girl to swear off makeup and boys forever.* You're curious, right? So you walk over and the student is explaining her procedures for testing waterproof mascara and the results of her study. She's not standing there awkwardly and you're not looking at some sort of decoupaged madness that her mother created. (*Note.* I have never tested mascara and cannot comment on the quality of Maybelline over other products. Please don't sue me.) The point is that you are hooking this girl into the nature of curiosity and getting her to buy in to the scientific procedure. You're valuing the experiment, not the product. And once she has the itch to answer more questions, you can add the additional necessary elements.

This also serves another purpose. Building interest is not something that can be done in isolation. Exposure to ideas breeds new ideas. That's why you're reading this book. You know I won't have all of the answers (although I'm really trying here), but I might trigger you to have an idea that will work for you and your students. So, by creating a situation where kids are begging for the details of an experiment, you are opening up little cracks in their brains for new ideas to bloom. Maybe you have to promote this "begging" by requiring them to rate the experiments based on the ones that had the best trigger statements, the most interesting findings, and that led them to ask the most "I wonder" questions.

That leads me to the second problem with a typical science fair. Kids have no idea what to study because we haven't cultivated curiosity in them. We always show up with a full day of lesson plans, backup plans, and that one activity in your bottom drawer just in case. We've been taught to be uber prepared, which is great. I mean, we do have standards to cover. But what if during a math lesson on statistics and probability, you have them figure out how they want to show you that they can apply the concepts you've taught them? Maybe they will choose to just create and complete a few word problems. Maybe Theo is really interested in the probability that the Los Angeles Lakers will win the championship, so he has to figure that out and present it to the class. Or, if you don't have time for that, he can present it to a small group, which can check his math.

What if you start every Tuesday of your math class with your students writing for 5 minutes as many "I wonder" statements that they can imagine? Maybe it's hard at first, but then, like any brainstorming, it becomes easier with practice. They may start by writing things like "I wonder why my parents are so strict" or "I wonder how I can get Kimberly to like me." But, once they know that this is an expectation and something your class regularly practices, they will brainstorm "I wonder" statements throughout their day, tucking them away to share with you. The frivolous evolves into "I wonder why Dr. K soda loses its fizziness faster than Dr. Pepper" or "I wonder how much difference recycling makes on the environment." You may argue that these aren't earth-shattering statements, but they certainly lead to more scientific studies. You are purposefully building curiosity in your students, which may be more important than some of the other things we focus on in school.

Utilizing Interest-Building Activities

Did you ever watch *Pop Up Video* on VH1? If you missed it in the 90s, go check it out. I love music and I was fascinated by this show. Little bubbles pop up every 10 seconds or so during the music video, giving you little nuggets of information about the artist, production of the video, the song, etc. It was like getting to know the music and artists I loved in a more personal way, like I was getting inside information. It was a musical version of "Did you know?"

So what if you had a weekly "Did you know?" session in your class? Maybe you introduce a topic you're interested in and share a few fun facts about it. The topic can relate to your content area or not. You model it a few times until your students want to share their fun facts. For example, did you know that there is a goat in

New Jersey with severe anxiety named Polly? Not so unbelievable. But do you know what calms Polly down? Wearing costumes. When Polly is dressed in her duck costume, she immediately relaxes (Lowin, 2016). Seriously, go look at her.

Incidentally, there are enough goats with special needs that Leanne Lauricella started a goat rescue farm to nurse and love on them. Now, at this point you should have some questions: What types of special needs can goats have? Are goat rescue farms common? What happens to the goats once they're rehabilitated? What started Leanne's quest to save these goats? You get the point. There's a chance that this activity leads your students down a rabbit hole of ideas and a quest for finding the fascinating in order to share it with other people.

If you've ever been trapped on a playground by a second grader, you know their little heads are full of interesting, sometimes useless, information. But although we think it's so cute in a second grader, we stop rewarding this habit as we get older. And, because there is no reward (like the rapt attention of your classmates), many students disengage from the discovery process. But by modeling and promoting this fascination with new information, students are more likely to be able to articulate the things they are interested in, while also deepening their understanding of the topic and (hopefully) triggering the interests of their peers.

Genius Hour, a theory of productivity that started at Google and gained momentum with *Drive* (Pink, 2011), is another way of giving structure to student interest-building activities. It's essentially a reborn version of independent study and can easily be implemented in individual classrooms or scaled to the entire school (Kesler, n.d.). It begins with a student-driven question that requires research to answer and ends with a sharing of a product. Ideally the "sharing" is with an authentic audience, but even sharing with the class brings authenticity to the project and potentially triggers the interests of the audience.

In her book *Genius Hour: Passion Projects That Ignite Innovation and Student Inquiry*, McNair (2017) outlined an easy-to-implement process for getting started with your students.

The key component to Genius Hour is that it originates with your students. And really, passion is highly personal, so it makes sense that students have that power. McNair's 6 P's of Genius Hour—passion, plan, pitch, project, product, and presentation—outlined in Figure 4 provide a framework for guiding your students through the process of developing their own passion projects.

Remember the Godfather of the Gifted, Dr. Renzulli? Renzulli and his colleague Sally Reis (2014) developed the Schoolwide Enrichment Model (SEM), a program with one overarching goal: to apply gifted education pedagogy to improve schools. Who doesn't want *that*? Ultimately, the smaller goals of SEM are to develop the talents of children by providing them with enriching and challenging experiences based on their interests. The focus of the SEM is to develop gifted behaviors in children based on their interests. Sounds a lot like the first step to building grit.

Renzulli's Enrichment Triad Model and SEM complement one another in how they ignite and develop students' interests. Remember that the Type I activities are more structured and oftentimes stem from what the teacher/school has organized. Type II activities fall within the SEM in that students are often grouped together to participate in enriching activities to explore and deepen their interest in a topic. Type III activities also fit within the SEM, but the clusters are made up of fewer students. Often at this point, students' interests are individualized and many work independently.

Implementing the SEM into a school can be intimidating, but Drs. Renzulli and Reis have developed a website full of resources for teachers and administrators from their 2014 book *The Schoolwide Enrichment Model: A How-to Guide for Talent Development* (3rd ed.) available at http://gifted.uconn.edu/schoolwide-enrichment-model/sem3rd. They provide a linear plan for developing an SEM that fits within your school, as well as everything you need for implementation. Seriously, it's not often that a researcher develops a model that is supported by more than 20 years of research and then provides practical steps to put it in place. That's why he's the Godfather.

Genius Hour 6 P's

1. **Passion:** What do you want to learn about? What do you think is interesting? What can you get excited about?

2. **Plan:** Who will be your outside expert? What materials will you need to complete the project? What will you need to do each day to reach your goals?

3. **Pitch:** How will you share your idea with the class? How will you get us on board?

4. **Project:** It's time to dive in! What do you need to do today to move forward with your project? What are you creating, making, or designing?

5. **Product:** What did you create? What can you show us to demonstrate your learning?

6. **Presentation:** How do you plan to share your learning? Can you share your idea or project with others? What tools will you use to make your presentation engaging for the audience?

FIGURE 4. *The 6 P's of Genius Hour. From* Genius Hour: Passion Projects That Ignite Innovation and Student Inquiry *(p. 16), by Andi McNair, 2017, Waco, TX: Taylor & Francis Group. Copyright 2017 by Taylor & Francis Group. Reprinted with permission.*

Encouraging Practice

In order to turn an interest into a passion, those interest-triggering activities need to happen over and over again. Remember that day when you fell in love? Whether you fell in love with your partner, a hobby, or pad Thai, the feeling of exhilaration is similar. The art of practice is placing yourself in opportunities so that you can feel this joy again and again.

Additionally, people who are gritty are never comfortable with what they've accomplished. They work daily to improve in their pursuit of excellence. They are also comfortable with their weaknesses and understand that they must attack these weaknesses in order to reach their goals (Duckworth, 2016). In addition to retriggering your interest through practice, you also must focus on improvement in order to reach your goals.

> The art of practice is placing yourself
> in opportunities so that you can
> feel this joy again and again.

Anders Ericsson is the psychologist credited for the 10,000-hour rule of exceptionality. His research on elite performers revealed that the best of the best practiced more than the really good and mediocre (as cited in Lebowitz, 2016b). However, he is careful to explain that it's not enough to just practice for 10,000 hours and then you're an expert. Your practice must be deliberate, focused on your weaknesses. And, he says, it's not very fun (as cited in Lebowitz, 2016c). This shouldn't surprise you. When was the last time you had fun listening to someone tell you that you weren't doing something good enough? But most of us can't imagine working on anything for that long if it isn't enjoyable. That is the difference between the really good and the best, the difference between gritty and not.

This kind of practice is rigorous and exhausting. So, while building your interest is fun, practicing takes a deep commitment to where you're going. It also takes a lot of time. So, if we are to promote this kind of practice in schools, we have to vertically align our interest-triggering activities. That means we have to take this interest-building business seriously, as seriously as we take our curriculum standards and standardized tests. It is really hard to become good at something if you change that "something" every year. Or if, because you are a busy/lazy seventh grader, you pick the same topic to explore every year. Either way, you never move to the next stage of interest development.

So, how do we do this? First of all, we set the expectation that we *will* find our content interesting. Think of it like a self-fulfilling prophecy. Or an "If we build it, they will come" philosophy. Second, we need to hold students accountable to building upon their prior interests. With technology today, it's easier than ever for students to create digital portfolios that can "travel" with them from year to year.

For example, let's talk about Brody, a third grader who loves football, particularly the Oakland Raiders. For his independent research project he chose to learn more about the players and the franchise. He created a product to showcase his learning to his peers. In fourth grade, his interests were similar, but he wanted to study Bo Jackson, arguably one of the best Raiders of all time. Because Brody's teacher believed in the power of vertically streamlining interest building activities, he required that Brody map out how his interests were related.

We have to take this interest-building business seriously, as seriously as we take our curriculum standards and standardized tests.

In fifth grade, Brody moved on to study other athletes who were skilled enough to play two professional sports, like Jackson. In sixth grade, he researched NCAA regulations, after being intrigued by Jackson's experience with the Tampa Bay Buccaneers. In the following year, Brody expanded his interests to how sports evolved into money-making businesses, and then sports marketing, and then how the media shapes our perceptions of professional athletes, and so on. . . . Each year, Brody's teachers required him to add his new topic to his interest map (see Figure 5); sometimes his interest was tangential to his prior year's interest, and other years the connection was more distant. Either way, he had to be able to articulate his choices.

What if Brody showed up in fifth grade and just could not stand the thought of studying anything related to football or sports one more year? That's okay. He would need to request a new interest map, and, again, be able to explain why the shift is necessary to the development of his interests. Then, when he goes to sixth grade and asked for a new topic *again*, his teacher could preview his interest maps to get a bigger picture of Brody's previous studies. This would help inform both Brody and his teacher as they make a decision for the current year.

Once more, this process is much easier with technology. Regardless of the system, the important thing is that this vertical alignment is crucial in building interest in our students. Industry leaders who value a task dedicate time to it; in this case, that means establishing a system that supports the ultimate goal of cultivating curiosity and fascination in our students.

Setting Goals

The practice should also be tied to what Duckworth (2016) called a stretch goal. (Remember Figure 1? Look back at page 7.) This is the kind of ceiling-crashing, door-opening, craziness we typically avoid when setting goals with students. As teachers, we want to focus on the practical and the achievable; the goal

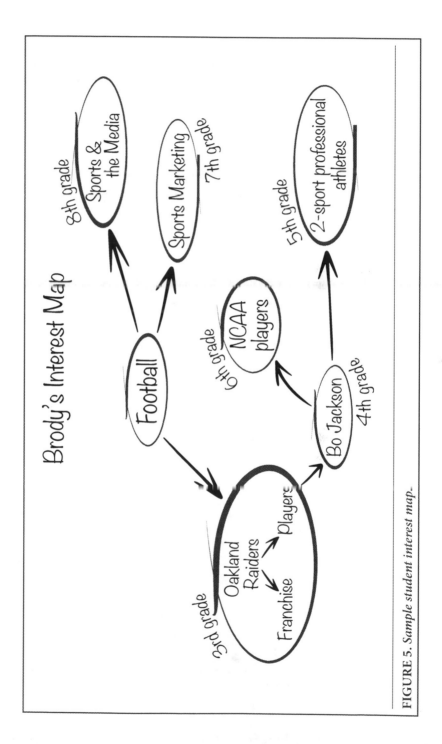

FIGURE 5. *Sample student interest map.*

has to be timely and specific, so that we can determine whether a student has met the goal at the end of the semester or year. But what if we had a big huge dream and then we were getting time to pursue that dream? At one point, I remember I wanted to be the first female President of the United States. Clearly, I had an interest in politics (and I thought the salary of the President sounded *uh-mazing*), but I also grasped, in some way, the idea of feminism. What if I were able to voice that to someone who would then help me figure out what I needed to do to get there? Would you be reading this book written by the United States President? No. But I surely would have learned a lot about politics, the "how to" of getting to be a world leader, and about feminists other than Susan B. Anthony (who was a #boss, but seriously there are a lot of amazing women out there that never made it into our token Women's History Month lesson). So, let's get crazy!

After articulating a stretch goal, we should let kids dive in headfirst. They should immerse themselves in the discipline until their interest is fully piqued and then we slowly shape this dive into purposeful practice. We need to require a great deal of effort and hold them accountable for learning and really getting to the heart of their interest, followed by giving them very specific and immediate feedback and asking them questions they can't answer. Their brains should *hurt* when their designated practice time is up and all synapses are firing with new information. And then we should give them time to reflect on their learning and outline their next steps. They (and you) end the day exhausted (#happyparents #happyteachers).

Identifying Purpose

Because persistence is such an integral part of grit, identifying a purpose is essential to maintaining focus. This purpose is what makes challenges bearable and is enough to sustain focus when you may want to give up. The purpose can be very specific (i.e., to learn everything I can about grit) or more broad (i.e., to contribute to the research in my field). Purpose is developed from a lot of factors, many outside of school, but typically has a strong tie to passion. I should also mention that purpose can be driven by hate or anger and one's purpose does not have to be altruistic; plenty of history's villains have been gritty with a definitive purpose. But they're not our focus here (#obviously).

Purpose is not easy to identify and it doesn't just "come to you." It may feel that way, when in actuality, your brain is processing all of the practice into something bigger, making connections to entities outside of yourself. It's then that you have your "ah-ha" moment.

The truth is that some of what we ask of children has no bigger purpose. Memorizing your multiplication tables will make your life easier in math, but isn't going to make you into a more admirable member of society. It will, however, help you understand how you learn and what kind of practice it will take you to memorize something in the future. That kind of self-awareness is invaluable and only results from experience and reflection. If we believe it's important to help children find their purposes, we have to provide/require experiences that allow them to make these connections.

Purpose is not easy to identify and it doesn't just "come to you."

As we help children develop interests into passions, we should also help them extend this into identifying their purposes. As they create their identities and establish who they are and what's important to them, they are also forming beliefs about why they are here and what they are going to do with their lives. Maybe someone could have asked me why I wanted to be the President. My first answer was that the salary sounded pretty sweet, but then later I might realize that I enjoy being in charge and, while I'm pretty introverted, I also lean toward leadership roles.

This deeper level of understanding doesn't just happen. As teachers, we need to help students dig deeper and, as sappy as it may sound, help them get to that emotional level where they are able to articulate the "why" behind their interests. Once there, they won't want to leave—even when you are enticing them with the greatest lesson of all time.

How do we do this? You start with a conversation, asking your student why she chose her topic. And then, like the most inquisitive toddler you've ever met, you will answer each response with a "Why?" (or perhaps something more cognitively stimulating) until you feel she has moved from the identification phase of the study to the purpose phase. You can do this 1:1 with each student or have students go through this process in pairs or small groups. It is important though, that you are aware of each student's ultimate why/purpose. Not only will this help you support your students, but it will inevitably result in building stronger relationships.

The truth is that finding a purpose is a philosophical quest that depends on the development of the child (or adult). It's also very personal and builds itself as part of the human experience. Our role in developing this component of grit should be similar to how a 3-year-old experiences life. Once students have established their interests, we should continually ask them to consider their choices. Over time, their answers will change as they mature, but our question should stay the same: Why?

Cultivating Hope

Hope is the thing with feathers

—Emily Dickinson

Hope may be the most important element of grit because it is layered over interest, practice, and purpose. In order to pursue excellence despite challenges, you have to believe that these challenges will wane and that eventually you will come out on top.

Hope in the context of grit is different from the hope that comes with luck, just as it's one thing for a 16-year-old to say, "I hope my parents get me a new car," versus, "I hope my studying for that chemistry test pays off." One is a shot in the dark—the teenager has no reason to believe he will actually be getting a new car—while the other is a product of his practice.

Duckworth (2016) suggested that hope accompanies a feeling of power. If you feel in control of your success and where you're headed, you're more likely to feel hopeful than if it feels like a crapshoot. Hopeful people are optimistic. When they see that they are failing or not doing very well, they face their weaknesses and make a plan for improvement. But let's face it, you're a teacher. You already know what hope is and it's likely the only thing that gets you out of bed some mornings. You believe in yourself and in your students that you can do better than yesterday.

If you're familiar with Carol Dweck's (2006) work and Mary Cay Ricci's (2013) book *Mindsets in the Classroom*, then you're probably screaming "mindset" at this book right now. Hope is absolutely tied to mindset, and we will explore how grit and Dweck's theory complement one another in Chapter 4 (#holdyourhorses).

> The key is to acknowledge what you cannot control in your students' lives. And then create experiences that allow them to achieve mastery amidst the struggle.

Maier and Seligman (1976) conducted a really interesting experiment with his graduate students (even though it does make me sad because it involves rats and I'm a softie. Carrying on . . .). One group of rats was subjected to electric shocks and could turn them off by completing a task. The other group of rats was also shocked, but could not turn them off. The rats were initially tested at 5 weeks old and then again when they were adults. Here's the interesting part: The rats who had no control over their shocks grew up to be timid; even if they could stop the shocks as adults, they behaved fearfully. The rats who had control over their shocks as adolescents were more resilient and spunky as adults even if they didn't have control over the shocks anymore. Now substitute the rats for kids and the shocks for something you have a bit of influence on—failure in school. If the child feels helpless early on, this grows into a learned helplessness as an adolescent.

Allowing Students to Struggle Yet Succeed

The key is to acknowledge what you cannot control in your students' lives. And then create experiences that allow them to achieve mastery amidst the struggle. That's how we grow to believe in ourselves. That's how we turn hope from being a "luck thing" to being an "I've got this" thing. This kind of power is, well, powerful in changing behavior. Creating these experiences is absolutely not easy. You have to be aware of your students' strengths and weaknesses (while you're also balancing a bazillion other tasks). You have to know how hard to push, when to back off, and how to differentiate your expectations based on their capabilities.

That's not easy, right? Luckily, you are a teacher, which means you're also an unlicensed psychologist with enviable intuition! You know when Billy comes to class ready to work and when Amanda does not. And when you don't know, you've established such a trusting relationship that you can just ask them (#nopressure). You see, the activities required to enhance the grit in your students are difficult. Your students will stay right there with you as long as they know that (1) you know what you're doing (and you do!) and (2) they trust that you care about them. It's really as simple as that. The good news is that you can have or develop #1; after all, you're reading this book. And you wouldn't be a teacher if you didn't have #2 ('cuz you surely aren't doing this for the glitz and glam).

This is when we talk about equity. I was fully committed to the idea of differentiation as a beginning teacher. I lived and breathed

Carol Ann Tomlinson's (2014) text and looked at every assignment as an opportunity to modify it to fit the needs of my learners. Some lessons were modified by content—one student read *Night* by Elie Wiesel (2006) while another read *Number the Stars* by Lois Lowry (2011). I differentiated others by process, which can be done in a couple of ways. One is to allow students to access content in the manner they prefer (i.e., through a video, audio clip, text, etc.). But the other, and the method I used more often, was by scaffolding the process more for students who needed it. For example, I provided specific graphic organizers to the students who struggled developing an idea into an essay, when other students might not have needed this step in this format. The third way to differentiate a lesson was the method my students preferred the most because it gave them choice. By differentiating the product, students could choose to create a presentation, write a short story, or develop a public service announcement. All students were required to address the content and all were held accountable to a rubric, but the "how" varied based on student choice.

> Your students will stay right there with you as long as they know that (1) you know what you're doing (and you do!) and (2) they trust that you care about them.

I worked ridiculously hard to create differentiated writing assignments for my eighth graders, only to hear someone whine, "Why do I have to write an entire essay when she gets to write just one paragraph?" Clearly this student had no appreciation for how hard I worked to be sensitive to my students' needs and didn't notice my slow blink as I tried to teleport her out of the room. I wish that I had explained the concept of equity to that class. I would have told them that we all have different interests and needs and that some lessons would reflect those differences. I would have also explained that there is no "privilege" related to how much or how little I asked them to write.

When I was in Girl Scouts, I went to a horseback riding camp. I loved horses and was convinced that I would own a horse one day, so I was thrilled when my mom sent me to this camp. On the first day, the counselor explained that she was dividing us into groups based on how advanced we were. I was crushed to find out that I was placed in the inexperienced group. (Truth be told, I had never ridden a horse before, but I was convinced I had some undiscovered talents.) Surprisingly (and this still makes no sense to me), in the inexperienced group, we were taught how to do tricks on the horses. I learned how to stand up, arabesque, and do a variety of dance moves—all while standing on a horse—a real-life, moving horse. I know what you're thinking—I'm the lucky one! I mean, the other girls learned to trot and other kinds of fast moves, but I was a horse gymnast. I don't know enough about horseback riding psychology to state this definitively, but I believe the counselor understood that beginning riders benefit from establishing trust with the horse and learning how to comfortably balance on the horse's back. I do know that I left camp feeling like I could do anything, on or off a horse. Clearly that's what I needed more than I needed to be treated the same as the advanced riders.

Although we've taught students like this, children who need confidence before content, we can't ignore the student who *never* struggles in school. He has no reason to have hope because he hasn't needed it yet. He's always made his parents proud and he's won all kinds of academic awards. His teachers love him, and his peers beg him to be in their groups for collaborative assignments. But you, yes, you, are doing him a disservice by not creating adverse experiences for him. You haven't required him to set a stretch goal. He will practice, but that rarely results in exhaustion. His commitment to any interests is minimal. You're allowing him to settle into complacency. More on this in the next chapter.

Final Thoughts

I have no special talents. I am only passionately curious.
—Albert Einstein

Building interest, establishing time to practice, and finding purpose are at the heart of developing talent. We build interest by creating classrooms that are places where students identify their passions and are rewarded for their curiosity. We help our students set goals aligned to practice, and we insist that our students find meaning in their studies. And pervading all of this is hope, the hope that our students need to dream big and believe in their ability to succeed.

Discussion Questions

1. Consider Bloom's (1985) stages of talent development. How do you support each stage (i.e., interest, practice, and purpose) in your classroom/school?
2. Reflect on the activities in your classroom/school. Which of these only require compliance? Of those, which can be more effective by emphasizing engagement over compliance?
3. How can you authentically build hope in your students?

Chapter 3

What Gritty Classrooms Can Learn From Gifted Education and Talent Development

I taught language arts to gifted eighth graders for most of my career. I didn't know much about how or when they were identified, nor was I aware if their "giftedness" was in my discipline. It didn't matter in my district; if a boy qualified as gifted in kindergarten, he maintained that status and was eligible for all gifted services until he graduated. My students exhibited a range of interests and expertise in language arts; some were productive and engaged, while others skated by with minimal mental investment. This didn't bother me at all because I recognized that something else (perhaps motivation?) was influencing their performance in my class. I also realized that they would be interested in reading, writing, and speaking regardless of their abilities. I saw my role as one who could bring life and passion to our studies so that I could

DOI: 10.4324/9781003235385-3

open minds and ignite fires. I was a living, breathing cliché, and it was great.

However, I also felt protective over my students. When talks surfaced of creating one language arts class made up of all levels of students that would be differentiated, I fiercely argued that this would be to the detriment of the gifted kids. When a faculty member would snarkily mumble, "He's gifted? Hmph," I would stand up for that student like I had brought him into this world myself. I knew these kids needed something different from what was offered in the on-level, and even honors, courses. But I was wrong.

This chapter will focus on talent development and the necessity of grit to this model of gifted education. It will also explain the role of grit in addressing social-emotional needs of gifted students and what all gritty classrooms can learn from the field of gifted education.

A New Direction for Gifted Education

I realized I was wrong in 2011. I attended the National Association for Gifted Children's (NAGC) annual conference in New Orleans, LA. Just as many had done before, Paula Olszewski-Kubilius delivered her presidential address to conference attendees. Now, if you've ever been to a conference where someone on the Board of Directors speaks, it can be a bit of a snooze. But that November, there was not a snooze to be had.

I didn't know it at the time, but 2011 was a big year for gifted education.

Olszewski-Kubilius unveiled a new definition of what it meant to be gifted. Up until that point, giftedness was considered to be something you were born with, a stable trait that led to some kind of exceptionality. Giftedness was also described as having the potential that would lead to excellence. It was difficult to explain what it meant to be gifted, which made it nearly impossible to accurately measure. Despite the difficulty, it's what we did for years.

I didn't know it at the time, but 2011 was a big year for gifted education. Three significant events took place around the same time and if you were paying attention, you might have even sensed the ground shifting.

1. NAGC published a white paper titled "Redefining Giftedness for a New Century: Shifting the Paradigm" (2010). In it, the organization reflected its stance on giftedness:

   > Gifted individuals are those who demonstrate outstanding levels of aptitude (defined as an exceptional ability to reason and learn) or competence (documented performance or achievement in top 10% or rarer) in one or more domains. Domains include any structured area of activity with its own symbol system (e.g., mathematics, music, language) and/or set of sensorimotor skills (e.g., painting, dance, sports). (para. 1)

2. Rena Subotnik, Paula Olszewski-Kubilius, and Frank Worrell (2011) published a paper titled "Rethinking Giftedness and Gifted Education: A Proposed Direction Forward Based on Psychological Science." In it, they offered this comprehensive definition:

   > Giftedness is the manifestation of performance or production that is clearly at the upper end of the distribution in a talent domain even relative to that of other high-functioning individuals in that domain. Further, giftedness can be viewed as developmental, in that in the beginning stages, potential is the key variable; in later stages,

achievement is the measure of giftedness; and in fully developed talents, eminence is the basis on which this label is granted. Psychosocial variables play an essential role in the manifestation of gift-edness at every developmental stage. Both cogni-tive and psychosocial variables are malleable and need to be deliberately cultivated. (p. 7)

3. Paula Olszewski-Kubilius gave her presidential address to the 2011 NAGC conference attendees focusing on this shift in how giftedness is perceived.

It's possible that you don't appreciate this mic drop moment, so let me remind you of my passion for gifted education. I loved and protected my gifted students. I pushed them to perform at their best, but I would never suggest that one of them didn't belong in my class. You could give me a room full of underachievers and I would spend the year back flipping my way through the curricu-lum, trying to incite them to do something, anything. I believed in them and never gave up.

But these new definitions were suggesting that I stop backflip-ping so that I could focus on the performers and producers. In my mind, I saw that as turning my back on the Joes and the Jessicas, students I loved dearly but did nothing (#blesstheirhearts). I just couldn't support this.

Evidently, sometimes passion can turn into crazy because I lost my mind at one point. My husband, who is a gifted education scholar, and I fought like we were on a reality television show. He used tricks like logic and reason to try to convince me that this definition was exactly what the field needed to be relevant. I had no need for these explanations because all I could think of were those kids who just might (maybe?) do the assigned reading one time. We didn't speak for days.

I was wrong in how I defined *gifted*.

In my quiet moments, I thought carefully about how transformative this new definition could be. The truth is, Joe and Jessica may not be as passionate as I am about language arts. (Gasp.) Perhaps they would be better served taking a less rigorous language arts course so they could focus on pursuing their passions in a different course. Or perhaps they would wake up and start performing because they were just being lazy and didn't realize they needed to step it up. But you know what else? This would also allow me to teach a student who was a prolific reader/writer, but not labeled "gifted" under the traditional model and take her to the next level.

In essence, by focusing on producers and performers, we are attributing great value to passion and perseverance. And, because our attention aligns to our values, we can now cultivate these skills so they are equipped to overcome the challenges along the way to eminence. So my heart was in the right place and my belief that gifted students need something different was correct; I was wrong in how I defined *gifted*.

Building grit in gifted students looks similar to building grit in all students: inciting passion and building their capacity to persevere through challenges. However, it is the *kind* of perseverance that can be different for gifted learners.

Giftedness and Grit

Identifying who is gifted and who is not is tricky business and I'm not here to debate a position on how this should be done. I do believe, however, in a funnel approach to talent development. That is, we should start with a large pool of individuals who demonstrate potential and then funnel that toward greatness. What if the people with the magic wand spent less time determining who was and was not gifted and more time on how we can maximize our time with our students, nurturing their potential? I understand that in an educational system, we need objective measures to identify those who will be served in our gifted program, but we don't need to capitulate to the limitations inherent in standardized methods. In addition to achievement tests, NAGC (n.d.) also recommends the use of nominations, observations, and student portfolios in identification, measures that can more likely capture one's potential.

Another important consideration, specifically in the context of building grit within a talent development framework, are the following four tenets recommended by Olszewski-Kubilius, Subotnik, and Worrell (2015).

1. Ability

First of all, ability matters. This ability can be general, in terms of outstanding performance on an achievement test, or specific to a domain. Importantly, the authors (Olszewski-Kubilius, et al., 2015) argued that ability is malleable. NAGC (n.d.) officials echoed this same sentiment when they suggested on their website that "giftedness is dynamic" (para. 2).

Ability matters.

I studied liberal arts and education my entire life. I loved it, but had never really faced an academic wall I wasn't sure I could climb. Well, as one does when going through a major life change, I cut my hair and enrolled in a doctoral program in research, measurement, and statistics. I didn't even really know what statistics were beyond the sports related stats I heard on television, which is exactly why I chose it. I'm sure my GRE scores were unfortunate on the math section—I've since blocked that out—but they let me in. I started slowly and studied hard. With specific training from excellent professors, my mathematics ability absolutely increased. I do not think I am in any way gifted, but I do know that with focused study and practice, growth happens.

2. Domain

Second, the trajectory of talent development varies by domain. The development of certain talents can be dependent upon physical maturity, while the development of other talents may begin earlier. This is important to understand because it can influence how performance and potential are measured. Perhaps "potential" is more important in instances where peak performance typically occurs later in life. In fact, all domains begin with potential and then move to competency and possible eminence.

All domains begin with potential.

My 11-year-old son is an athlete in all parts of his little body. Unfortunately for him, he takes after my height (5'1" . . . okay, fine, 5') and not his dad's (6'2"). So, while he is quick and tough as nails, he's small. He was dying to play football, so we signed him up. You know what bothered him the most? It wasn't that he was getting tackled by boys who weighed as much as me or that he had to deal with the insane Texas heat on the football field. It was that he didn't get the ball very often. He was a free safety and made some great plays, but he was not going to be a receiver or quarterback until he grew. So, he switched to soccer and continues to pursue baseball. His talents clearly lie in athletics, but his growth trajectory was not ideal for football. Thank goodness.

3. Opportunities

The third tenet is that children must be exposed to opportunities throughout the entire talent development process. Not only does this build students' interests, but they can begin to see where their talents can take them if they continue pursuing them. As students' abilities and interests grow, the opportunities they need to further their development will change. This gets trickier as they move beyond initial practice to establishing more of an expertise.

> As students' abilities and interests grow, the opportunities they need to further their development will change.

When he was in eighth grade, I taught a very gifted mathematician. Mark was extremely bright and was fortunate enough to have parents who supported his passion for math. They knew how to support him and knew who to ask when they needed help. They allowed him to finish his last 2 years of high school at a math and science academy for gifted mathematicians. During that time he earned more than 50 college credits and regularly outperformed the college students in his classes. He is currently pursuing an advanced degree in mathematics, publishing in academic journals regularly, and posting things on Facebook that I don't understand. What if Mark's parents weren't educated? What if they didn't have the resources to support his pursuit of math? This is where we need to step in. There is no way I was equipped to support Mark's pursuit of math, but I could have found him a mentor. I could have set up an internship for an elective. I could have made sure he took advantage of every opportunity we had to offer him and made sure he was on track to earn scholarships. My fear, however, is that these Marks are shuffled through the system and are living dramatically different lives than my Mark with his sophisticated Facebook posts.

4. Psychosocial Skills

Fourth, psychosocial skills, particularly grit, are necessary to the talent development process. When we think of the previous tenets of talent development (i.e., ability, developmental trajectory, and opportunity), we know that a constant will be the presence of obstacles. Without the resilience, hope, and persistence that accompany grit, it is difficult to overcome the doubt and fear that naturally occur amidst setbacks.

Psychosocial skills, particularly grit, are
necessary to the talent development process

The Necessity of Grit in Gifted Education

I taught in a school district known for the quality of its education. The housing market reflects this, as houses sell for the asking price or above within days of being listed. The gifted program has changed some over the years, but has been pretty solid at the elementary, middle, and high school levels. The parents in this community tend to be educated and professional with high expectations for their children.

Despite this, I ran into a variety of obstacles when trying to challenge the students in my gifted language arts class. I realize that some of these challenges are not unique to gifted learners, but they are important to include in this discussion. Furthermore, although I'm discussing students here, their parents often behaved similarly. You know who I'm talking about.

Here is a shocking truth: Some students in my class only cared about their grades. They did not value learning if that meant it would cost them points toward their average. I dreaded the last week of the grading period because my inbox would be full of messages from parents and students asking about make-up work, reassessments, extra credit, or just asking for a bump to the next grade. Students would be waiting outside my door and would come to me with tears in their eyes because of their grades. For many of these eighth graders, the B they earned in my class was their first.

We take away the easy button, and we demand,
while we also encourage, earned excellence.

What was happening here? With their eyes only on their grades, they missed the big picture. This meant that they were able to demonstrate mastery, and sometimes excellence, on scaffolding lessons for the first part of the grading period. However, when required to apply this knowledge in a new context, they were unable to perform at the expected level. And then they panicked. They didn't know what it meant to work hard intellectually.

This is why grit is so important to cultivate in our gifted learners. They should know, from the very beginning of their academic careers, what it's like to work hard. They should understand how to struggle through difficult content *and* they should firmly believe in their abilities to persevere through these challenges. We know that they will only do this if we require it of them, right? They're kids. They will take the easy road if we offer it, so what do we do? Don't offer it. We take away the easy button, and we demand, while we also encourage, earned excellence.

Talent Development in Sports and Academics

When I married my husband, I was blessed to become a stepmom to four children. One of our boys plays competitive baseball. And by "competitive," I mean expensive—both in time and money. But it was an amazing experience that none of us would take back. While carpooling him, cheering for him, and making him ice packs, I saw firsthand what happens when passion intersects with perseverance. He regularly missed family vacations and outings with friends for baseball. He broke his face, literally, and couldn't wait to buy a guard for his helmet so he could get back out on the field. There were few things that could get him out of bed on a Saturday before noon, but baseball was one of them. He was, and still is, gritty in a way that I have rarely seen. And his team was full of other boys just like him.

This is what *talent development* looks like. He has one passion and he makes all of his decisions in order to get him closer to his dream of playing in the majors. Even with setbacks, he continues to come back to his stretch goal. He's in college now, and nothing gets the time and attention that he gives to baseball. Not hanging out with friends, not dating, not his classes, not watching TV. Nothing.

I believe that we need to develop academic talent like we develop athletic talent.

His coach, like coaches of all elite teams, understands the system of talent development. Coaches begin with a bunch of kids with varying levels of talent, commitment, and passion for the game. When the players are young, coaches are focused on developing skills while keeping the fun alive. As players grow, coaches create experiences that build players' mental toughness, their ability to cope with pressure in order to achieve their goals. And what helps them cope? That's right: grit.

I believe that we need to develop academic talent like we develop athletic talent. Coaches have had this thing figured out forever and have quite a system. Kettler (2016) outlined seven principles for how coaches create world-class players with the goal of transferring this system to other domains. The first three principles are driven by the goal of the program:

1. the goal should be explicitly stated,
2. the goal should be bold and should focus on supreme levels of achievement, and
3. the goal should be the rationale for every program-related decision. In terms of schools, we can see how these beliefs can transfer (p. 7).

It is likely that most school districts can check off principles one and three; however, it's the "boldness" and the "supreme levels of achievement" that I doubt. It's not easy to be bold in public education. But neither is adulting, and we do that every day. Most days. Qualifying a record number of national merit scholars and reporting high SAT and ACT scores are great, but I don't think they count as being "supreme." Supreme achievement is when you cannot go any higher. You've reached eminence. (I know you're doubting me right now, but I'll come back to this.)

The remaining four principles (Kettler, 2016) focus on the players:

1. the players try out annually,
2. the players are coached as though they will reach eminence,
3. the players understand that they need discipline and commitment and that they will be provided with intensive support along the way, and
4. the players singularly focus on this one area (p. 7).

These, like the first three principles, are tricky.

First, the annual tryout. Consider how this would look in your gifted program. In mine, it would probably involve so much paperwork that I would start considering a career change. But let's imagine that the administrators in charge have designed a stream-lined process. From the students' perspective, it could be a pretty stressful time for them. Can you imagine sweet Kenneth who was gifted in first grade, but not in second? No way would we do that to Kenneth, right? Remember that we want to identify as many people as possible who will take us to the supreme level of achievement. Instead, we make sure that Kenneth is given the opportunities to excel in the areas where he demonstrates ability and potential. Perhaps when he "tries out" for the gifted language arts class, his teacher recognizes that he is better suited to be challenged in science. His ability has crystallized a little more between first and second grade; shouldn't his education reflect that? Especially if we want to cultivate passion and exceptionality? It doesn't mean that he still can't enjoy language arts and it doesn't mean that he's "stuck" with gifted science curriculum. Think of the gifted program as a constant reshuffling of kids according to their achievement and potential; as they develop, where they fit changes. That's fantastic.

It's our job to help our students focus their passion in order to achieve as much as possible.

Second, we recognize that most of our students will not reach the supreme level of achievement that is stated in our program goal. (I told you I would come back to this.) But, just because we know that Kenneth won't reach that level does not mean that we won't teach him like he will. Ask any high school football coach what his goal is. It's likely that he will mention winning the state championship. It doesn't matter if his team is a ragtag group of scrawny boys he recruited from the recycling club; his goal is the same and he will coach those boys as if they will win. Every under-dog success story is a success because there were no limitations placed upon them. It's not our job as teachers to put limitations on what our students can accomplish; it is, however, our job to help our students focus their passion in order to achieve as much as possible.

This brings me to Kettler's (2016) third principle. If we have a bold goal for our gifted program and we are supporting each student as though he will be the next Sylvia Plath or Thomas Jefferson, we also need to help our students understand the commitment that supreme achievement entails. They will have to practice, face obstacles, and persevere even when they want to quit. But we have equipped them with mentors and performance opportunities along the way that will cultivate their passions to such intense levels that they can't fathom quitting. They love what they're doing and they believe in the dream.

Finally, students must prioritize their focus in their talent area, which means they won't be able to be as committed to other areas. We saw this with Kenneth earlier; he demonstrated more talent in science than in language arts, so his intense focus should be on science. That doesn't mean that he won't be challenged in reading, writing, and speaking, but it does mean that the intensity and expectations will not be the same.

Classroom Application

Every single gifted student needs to be regularly and appropriately challenged. At this point you may be thinking, "Duh. All students need to be challenged." If you're thinking that, you're correct. But did you know that there are folks out there who think gifted kids don't need anything different from their nongifted peers? There are! I've heard comments like, "I have too many kids who need help that I can't spend time on the gifted ones," or "The gifted kids will be fine anyway," or "My gifted students are the tutors who work with my strugglers." You get the point. Now, all of these points are hinting at a very valid concern: We are stressed out about not having the resources we need to help our struggling students, let alone those who can already read/write/insert action verb here. Despite this, I am going to repeat my main point for this section because, as an advocate for cultivating grit in *all* students (even those who don't seem like they need it), it is so essential: Every single gifted student needs to be regularly and appropriately challenged.

Regular challenges mean often. Every day. Along with these regular challenges is that students need immediate feedback. If you teach like a coach, you are giving constant feedback to reinforce the behaviors you want to see. This is one of the most challenging aspects of being a teacher. It's not easy to give immediate feedback when you are dealing with the hundreds of responsibilities you have on top of your actual job. Your class sizes are huge, you're dealing with behavior issues, you're filling out paperwork, you're attending meetings that really should be e-mails, and on and on. I get it. But we have to figure this out.

How? Force your students to "perform" regularly. Be as random as possible—call on students at all points during the day or class period. Create an environment where your gifted students know they are responsible for knowing the material. These can be quick assessments that don't require higher level thinking; the point is that they learn to be "on" so that they aren't blindsided when asked to perform at deeper levels. And coach them when they need to improve.

Force your students to "perform" regularly.

And then require them to change. Let's go back to baseball. When I watched my son in the batting cage, his coach would tell him to raise his back elbow. (Evidently this is an important maneuver.) Then, he would pitch to my son again, and, again, his elbow would be too low. So the coach would repeat the instruction. And repeat it and repeat it. If my son would drop his bat in a huff, I would see the coach walk calmly toward him, put his hand on my little boy's shoulder, and give him a talk to cool him down. Then, they would get back at it. The coach would not excuse my son from the batting cage until he demonstrated that he could complete the task that was asked of him.

Why then, did I spend hours writing comments on essays, giving students detailed feedback on their writing, and then never hold them accountable for those specific mistakes? Most likely, it was because I couldn't stand to read those essays one more time. Kidding. Sort of. Why did my daughter's math teacher send home a graded quiz at the end of the unit with no accountability for fixing her mistakes? I'll tell you why. Because it's hard. And teachers are tired. But, here is the good news. What if we focus this kind of feedback on those who have demonstrated the ability and potential in our discipline? Remember that we are shuffling kids around regularly, per Kettler's (2016) fourth principle. Sure, we are going to work with all students, but we are really pushing those ones with the ability and potential to reach a supreme level of achievement. That's more manageable, right? It's certainly more rewarding. Plus, by not having as high of expectations for the other students, you aren't killing the fun for them. And who knows, they may shuffle back to your gifted course after the next tryout.

> ## Focused energy brings a more powerful response than energy sprayed out in several directions.

Remember that I suggested that students are *appropriately* challenged. First of all, the more passionate you are about something, the more likely you are to endure challenges. This means that when gifted students get to the "practice" stage of developing passion, they should be more focused on a specific discipline. Before fully committing to baseball, my stepson played all other sports. However, when approaching the next level of practice, he focused his attention on the sport where he was talented and passionate. And although he endured a lot from his coach, he would not have welcomed the same rigorous expectations from his science teacher, youth pastor, or recreational basketball team. And because he was focused on building excellence in just one area, he was more successful. It's physics, right? Focused energy brings a more powerful response than energy sprayed out in several directions.

To translate this into our stages of developing passion, you can think of Stage 1 as exploration. This goes on as long as necessary until interest has been established. Typically students move to Stage 2 in middle school, with a narrowed focus on a definitive passion. The final stage, finding purpose, begins in young adulthood and often develops alongside maturity. For gifted learners, this process may occur at a quicker pace.

By the end of my time in the classroom, I had also dealt with numerous issues of cheating. Most of the time this was because they weren't prepared. You're probably thinking, "Duh," but hear me out. It wasn't that they weren't prepared for the assessment. It was that they weren't prepared to be challenged. They, and their parents, were used to them earning good grades without putting forth much effort. So once they were in a situation where they had to work hard, they didn't know how to handle it. And they didn't want to lose the "giftedness" that made them unique.

Identity and Grit

Gifted students struggle with establishing an identity. Not only do they have to overcome potential cultural and gender stereotypes, they sometimes have to choose between being accepted and being talented. For example, minority students who are identified as gifted often struggle as they try to blend their academic and social worlds (Grantham & Ford, 2003). In many instances, they find themselves in positions where they need to choose between social acceptance and academic challenge. Gifted girls also struggle—their interests are similar to gifted boys, but they experience social-related stress from trying to fit in with other girls (Kerr & Multon, 2015). Boys, particularly gifted creative boys, also grapple with balancing their interests while conforming to peer pressure related to masculinity.

The most fortunate gifted students are those who were lauded for their accomplishments by their peers, but I'm sure we all can describe a handful of students who weren't. Perhaps they were teased or used by their peers; even worse, they may have been excluded entirely as if their existence was immaterial. What are we supposed to do with these kids? How are we supposed to support them?

We need to remember that gifted individuals develop asynchronously. Essentially this means that they may develop in one area (i.e., cognitive, physical, or emotional) at a different rate than they develop in another area. For example, a 5-year-old may worry deeply about childhood homelessness to the point where she gives away her belongings and refuses to sleep in her bed, but she is not potty trained. A high school student may be a lab assistant in a genetics lab at a local university, but has no concept of current events. You can imagine that this disparity between what gifted individuals can do in one domain versus what they cannot in another causes some issues in how they are accepted by their peers.

For many gifted students, their identities are centered on their giftedness, in a pretty irrational way.

This is why, even within a talent development framework, we must appreciate that gifted individuals require different support than their peers. To begin, they need to understand what is going on with them so that they can process and make sense of it. Furthermore, we have to recognize that, while gifted students share a similar label, they are unique and should be treated accordingly. Whether a procrastinator or a perfectionist, gifted students require services that are different from the average student. It's for these kids that we should cast a wide net for finding all of the gifted ones. That is, we should work to identify those with outstanding ability and/or the potential for excellence and provide the social and emotional support they need, particularly as they form their identities.

For many gifted students, their identities are centered on their giftedness, in a pretty irrational way. Hannah and a group of her friends would eat lunch in my classroom, and we would talk about things that bothered them. One issue that came up was this idea of identity being tied to ability. For example, Hannah always excelled in math. She grasped concepts quickly and her scores were always at the top of her class. She and her friends would tell each other their scores on math tests immediately after they were passed back, thereby creating a community of braggarts. Hannah was upset one day because she earned a lower grade on a test than she expected (probably a B) and her friends were shocked. Some bragged, "I'm smarter than Hannah," and teased her relentlessly. She was devastated because math was her thing, and if she didn't have this thing, if it could be taken from her in an instant, then who was she?

> Our place in education is to create experiences that are valued—experiences that cultivate passions, provide challenges, and leave room for failure.

Forming an identity is a social endeavor. A child looks around, assigns values to certain behaviors he sees in those around him, and begins to shape who he wants to be. He's influenced by family, friends, and any number of societal factors. Our place in education is to create experiences that are valued—experiences that cultivate passions, provide challenges, and leave room for failure. We want him to recognize that he's gifted in music, but that he's still gifted despite setbacks. We want him to value the demands placed upon him so that how he responds to those becomes part of his identity. Sure, he may be a musician, but he's also compassionate, determined, and (I hope) gritty.

Lessons to Apply to General Education

Okay, so we don't all teach gifted kids. I get that, but there is still so much we can learn about how to approach all students based on what we know about our gifted learners. Are you ready?

The first, and most important, point I want to make is this: We have to stop focusing on the labels we assign to our students. Read that again, and then let me explain.

Labels are important for really one reason: They allow us to identify what our students need and how we can support them. Jordan has dyslexia? Got it. Ramon has ADHD? Check. Brianna has an auditory processing disorder? Roger that. You see, we use these labels to help us understand how we can support our students best. It makes total sense. But I always get so frustrated when I learn about how much time and resources are spent on identifying who is gifted and who is not. If we think about our students in the talent development context, and if our goal is to develop elite performers, then the label no longer matters.

To ensure that I'm not misunderstood here and tweeted about as being antigifted, please let me remind you that gifted students absolutely have unique needs and that these needs must be understood and addressed by the people in their lives. However, I am advocating that we spend more time focused on developing talent than we do on being the gatekeepers. Being "gifted" should no longer be about having membership to an exclusive club, but instead be one of the ways we can describe a person.

> I'm arguing that it doesn't matter whether you are labeled as gifted or not—it's *what you do* that matters.

In many instances, it seems that being described as gifted is similar to being described as a unicorn. It's elusive and maybe even a little elitist. I'm arguing that it doesn't matter whether you are labeled as gifted or not—it's *what you do* that matters.

So let's talk about that. What are some universal concepts about grit that we can learn from the gifted world? First, we need to make "hard" the norm. All students at all levels need to be challenged daily and in every subject. As experts in our field, we should provide scaffolding and support to those who need it, but no longer will we hear our students whine about having to work hard as if it's out of the ordinary because it isn't. They will still complain, because that's part of their job description, but their complaints will be focused elsewhere.

Second, we need to help our students identify their talents and strengths in every domain and then encourage and push them to strive toward excellence in those areas. Maybe Janie really struggles in math, but for some bizarre reason has the Pythagorean theorem memorized. She can even explain it to the most novice of students in a way that you never could. Well, every time that theorem comes up, Janie is your expert and takes over the class to explain it. Is this "talent" going to change Janie's life? Probably not. But it will give her authentic confidence and opens doors to new theorems she might find interesting. That's a win, people.

In the bigger picture, we want Janie to understand where her true strengths lie. Sure, she's got the Pythagorean theorem in math, but that doesn't make her feel alive like writing poetry. Or playing softball. Or debating. Or singing. You get the picture. Depending on the development of your students, strengths may be viewed as interests. For example, Antonio may not be a great actor, but he loves being on that stage and spends all of his free time running lines. If we want to help our students perform at elite levels, we need to recognize their strengths.

Finally, we need to accept that we play a crucial role in helping all of our students establish their identities. We want a thousand things for our students, right? But to narrow those down, we want them to believe in their abilities, to know that they are worth more than a singular success or failure, and that with grit they can overcome obstacles. Those beliefs, not their labels, should be at the core of their identities.

Final Thoughts

Talent is never static. It's always growing or dying.
—Stephen King

If you line up all of the kids in the class, there is a really good chance that you can't pick out the gifted ones. You may be able to point out who is shy, who is goofy, who is nervous, but giftedness doesn't typically manifest itself physically. This is why it's easy for them to fly under the radar, and why you have to work even harder to make sure you are meeting their needs.

Developing talent is comprised of four components: ability, understanding the domain, providing opportunity, and building psychosocial skills. Although I briefly explained those first three in this chapter, my aim was to help you realize the importance of the last one, the psychosocial skills—particularly cultivating grit in all of your students.

Discussion Questions

1. What is going well, and what is not, in your gifted education program?
2. How does your school approach talent development, if at all? Are there steps you can take to develop academic talent in all of your students?
3. How can you improve the feedback you give to your students in order to challenge and hold them accountable?

Chapter 4

Integrating Grit, Mindsets, and Motivation

Okay, I need to be honest with you. Prior to writing this book, I was pretty tired of hearing about *mindset*. Buzzword overload. You know what was rubbing me the wrong way? It was hearing people describe the growth mindset like a slogan: *You can do anything if you put your mind to it.* That's great, and I can appreciate it as an optimist, but (as a realist) it's just not true. There are limits to what we can become and accomplish, and I found it annoying that people were twisting the theory into something it isn't. So, I'm here to help you understand what mindset theory really is, as well as goal orientation and how that can affect motivation. Even more, I'll offer ideas for how we can build capacity in our students to pursue mastery, and ultimately grit.

By this point in your life, you presumably understand that struggles and failure are natural experiences when striving for excellence. Someone who is gritty will likely persevere through these struggles. We know that in addition to the passion that leads one to pursue a goal, motivation is also important. What else is

DOI: 10.4324/9781003235385-4

there, besides grit, that is the difference between the person who gives up and the person who persists? Perhaps, it's one's mindset.

Fixed and Growth Mindsets

Carol Dweck is credited with deepening our understanding of mindsets. In her book *Mindset: The New Psychology of Success* (2006), she explained that a mindset is how we approach goals and challenges. Dweck suggested that mindset is merely a choice and that we have the ability to decide whether we embody a fixed or growth mindset. This is excellent news, people. Choices can be molded. Just like I can train myself to sit down and write every day, we can train our students to choose the optimum mindsets for success.

A *fixed mindset* is exactly that—it's fixed, static, rigid. It's believing that you either have "it" or you don't. The "it" can be football talent, intelligence, cooking ability, etc. Someone with a fixed mindset believes she was born with it and no amount of hard work/practice/commitment can change it. I taught so many students with this mindset. They would come into my honors language arts class and announce that they were terrible writers and really didn't even like to write. Once I dried my tears and pulled the stake from my heart, I tackled these beliefs daily. I would take these students who came to me in eighth grade (*eighth* grade!) with these attitudes about themselves and their abilities and would create waves of opportunities to change their minds. I was more successful in some cases than others, but I was trying to change attitudes they've had about themselves for years. Imagine if we focused on mindset early on, if we could cultivate students who didn't believe their "it" was stagnant.

A person with a growth mindset thrives on challenge and seeks out growth opportunities.

Enter the realm of the *growth mindset*, where students believe they can improve their skills through practice and hard work. Instead of walking into my room defeated, imagine students who knew they had work to do, and were ready to roll up their sleeves and get to it. That's a dream, right? A person with a growth mindset thrives on challenge and seeks out growth opportunities. She believes that, with effort, she can perform better, and that there is little about herself that she can't control. Tell me that you don't want a classroom full of those kids.

Dweck (2006) suggested that people take cues from the outside world about their mindsets. Growing up, I used to hate to hear people described as having "natural" talents. You know why? Because I didn't seem to have any. It is a humiliating experience to describe the number of athletic teams I tried out for, just hoping to be discovered by a coach and recognized for this latent ability I'd been hiding all these years. The type of sport was a nonissue; I merely wanted to be good at something. Finally in sixth grade, I was recognized by my language arts teacher for my writing. This was echoed again in ninth grade, and so on. I was praised by teachers for my ability to revise and refine my writing. So you know what? I entered writing competitions, read voraciously, and eventually became an English teacher. This was not a coincidence. I was absolutely shaped by the beliefs about me by those around me. You—yes, you—can be the teacher who highlights "it" or many "its" for your students. And, because you know the relationship between grittiness and success, you can foster the skills in your students that will lead to perseverance and cultivate passion.

I love the graphic in Figure 6. Take a look at it and think about where you fall in the different areas of your life. Think about your students and how they view the challenges, obstacles, effort, criticism, and success of others in your class. I like the logic of starting at a belief and ending with achievement. Perhaps you have a stu-

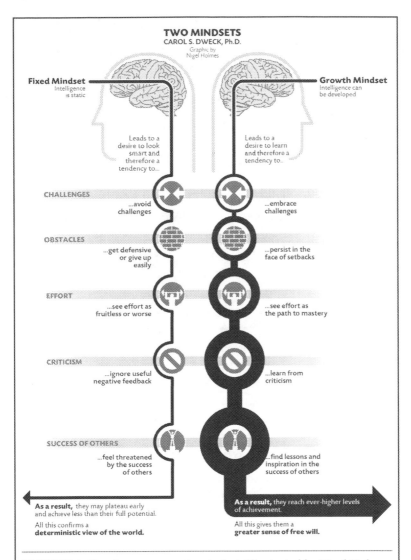

FIGURE 6. *Fixed versus growth mindset. Illustrated by Nigel Holmes. From "The Effort Effect" by M. Krakovsky, 2007,* Stanford Magazine, *36(2), p. 48. Copyright 2007 by Nigel Holmes. Reprinted with permission of the illustrator.*

dent who does embrace challenges, but then gives up as soon as it gets difficult. You can think of Nigel's diagram as a diagnostic tool to intervene and get your students (or yourself) back on track.

The Danger of a Fixed Mindset

While I was a teacher, I also sponsored our school's chapter of National Junior Honor Society (NJHS). The "honor" in the title referred to the character and academic performance required for membership. Over the years, my cosponsor and I noticed that our students were becoming more competitive with one another and were caught cheating more than ever before. There are all kinds of problems we could discuss here, but I want to highlight the relationship between having a fixed mindset and cheating. If a boy has been praised most of his life for his intelligence, that becomes part of who he is and, if he fears that intelligence is all he has, then he will go to any length to protect that image. He doesn't believe that he has any control over his performance in class; he's just always been the smart kid. Imagine a class full of students just like him, because they are sitting in the seats of our honors courses. And our remedial courses are full of students who don't believe they can "do" school because they have never seen returns on their hard work. Why do you suppose this is?

When you hear a coach describe his player as having the heart of a champion, he isn't referring to his performance in the gym or on the field—it's everything else that keeps him at the top of his game.

I propose that this is because they don't know how to work hard. Shocking, I know. As educators, we need to make hard work a habit. It's what we do. Another memory from my language arts class was my students whining every time I unveiled a new writing assignment. "Another project???" they would huff. More often than not, I would look at them incredulously—I know, I don't know why I was shocked every single time—and tell them, "This is language arts. We read, write, and think. Every day." Working hard should not be something students do because they have a big test coming up or because their average is almost high enough. We should make hard work a habit so that our students repeatedly experience positive effects as a result. This is how you change a fixed mindset to a growth mindset. It's also how you build grit.

My NJHS students didn't realize that, while ability can get them to the top, it's their tenacity, passion, and character that keep them there. When you hear a coach describe his player as having the heart of a champion, he isn't referring to the player's performance in the gym or on the field—it's everything else that keeps him at the top of his game. This is why the best coaches recruit players with potential. They aren't looking for players who have peaked with nowhere else to go. They're looking for the ones who fall and get back up, who push past their limits, and who work tirelessly to improve. They want the gritty ones who believe firmly that their success is a direct result of their hard work. Shouldn't we do the same in our classrooms?

Understanding a Growth Mindset

You've read my arguments throughout this book that the academic world can and should approach talent development similarly to the athletic world. And I'm not stopping yet. Dweck (2006) summarized the findings of sports psychologists who studied the mindsets of athletes and highlighted some interesting, yet not very shocking, truths. As you read these, consider whether these beliefs and behaviors would be welcome in your classroom.

We should make hard work a habit so that our students repeatedly experience positive effects as a result.

First, athletes with a growth mindset derive pleasure from practice, from rehearsing for the big performance. Second, they see their setbacks as arrows, pointing them toward weak areas in order to improve. And finally, they recognize the control they have over their performance and own it, rather than blaming other factors. These findings should be the base of our belief about what it means to be successful in any domain.

Additionally, a person's internal monologue clearly voices his mindset. If someone with a growth mindset misses a problem on a math test, he may chastise himself for the incorrect answer, but he also takes note of how to not repeat the mistake on a future test. It's not about whether he is "smart enough" to get a good grade; it's a recognition that he makes mistakes and has room for improvement. I think of my internal monologue as the voice of my self-esteem; sometimes it is an articulation of my insecurities or a proclamation of my awesomeness. Changing your internal monologue is another level of hard work; it requires dedication to quiet the negative voice and to spin the commentary into something more productive. This is a practice that should be *intentionally taught* at an early age and *regularly revisited*.

This is actually very easy to do! All you need to do is establish a routine of feedback after projects, tests, and other larger assignments. Ask students to describe how they are feeling about their grades and feedback. Then, have them identify what they did to earn their grades and what processes they controlled. Additionally, and importantly, ask them to determine what they could not control. Build in time for students to discuss their reflections with a partner.

You need to train your students in how to have these discussions. They need to face one another, knees to knees, so that they can also practice eye contact conversation etiquette. Partner 1 describes his reflection, and Partner 2 listens. Then, Partner 2 responds specifically to what Partner 1 could and could not control in preparing for the assignment. Imagine this conversation:

Partner 1: I'm pretty happy with my grade. I mean, I passed, and that's what matters. Last night I went to my friend's house to study and that helped a little, so I had control over that. What I didn't have control over, though, was that my parents made me come home for dinner and my sister's dance recital. It would have been nice to study more with my friend.

He starts with how he's feeling and then describes what he can/cannot control related to how he prepared.

Partner 2: That's great that you are happy about your grade. That's a good feeling. It's also nice that you have a friend you can study with. What about the recital? How much more did you need to study when you had to go home?

Partner 2 validates his partner's feelings and asks clarifying questions.

Partner 1: Well, we had pretty much covered everything, plus we were getting distracted FaceTiming with Tyler. But still, I wasn't ready to go home.
Partner 2: So, I'm hearing that you didn't have enough time to study because you were FaceTiming and had to go home earlier than you wanted. Is that right?

Partner 2 restates the issue.

Partner 1: Yeah.
Partner 2: What could you have done so you wouldn't have lost the time FaceTiming? Or is there a way you could have planned around the recital?

Note that Partner 2 doesn't offer solutions. Instead, he starts the brainstorming process. In doing this, Partner 1 is more likely to make different (hopefully better) choices in preparing next time because *he* came up with the ideas and they weren't just told to him.

The Power of the Experience

I've always been an optimist. I see a problem and find a solution because, in my mind, no problem is too big to solve. I don't get lost in the details and I don't get overwhelmed easily. I switch from dreamer to pragmatist and get down to the business of problem solving. However, I don't want to pretend like I've always been a fan of this mindset business. I've definitely struggled with the concept because, while I am an optimist, I believe there are limitations to our abilities.

> We need to practice optimism
> with our students if we want them
> to have a growth mindset.

Our thoughts are extremely powerful. That's a given. If I didn't think I could write a book, you wouldn't be reading this right now. If I didn't think I could get those abs I've always wanted, I wouldn't work out. The difference is that I understand that just thinking about those things won't make them happen. Sadly. I know there is a price to pay and a commitment to make. I also know that there is a good chance I won't get the abs I've always wanted. Why? Because I love pizza and cake. Because sometimes I want to binge watch TV instead of workout. I may have the positivity, but I don't have the *grit*. This is where teachers (and personal trainers) come in.

We need to practice optimism with our students if we want them to have a growth mindset. This is easiest to do if you've created a classroom climate that values the learning experience above all else. Consider the phrase "learning experience" for a moment. A typical teacher may suggest that the most important word is "learning." But you're not typical—you know the most important part of that phrase is "experience." At the risk of taking an existential dive, I ask you why else we are here on this planet? It's to live, to experience. Am I right? (#yesIam)

Once you, as the teacher, have placed the ultimate value on the *experience*, it no longer needs to be categorized as positive or negative. It's about what was felt and what we can learn from that experience. Once you have convinced your students that their experiences are uniquely theirs, you have given them stability in knowing that they matter. Everything they do matters. Each challenge should be welcomed because it will make for an exceptional experience. Each failure should be embraced because it will lead to extraordinary growth. I believe this is at the heart of Dweck's work and building a growth mindset.

Motivation and Goal Orientation

Raise your hand if you wish your students were more motivated? Yeah, me too. When I was a beginning teacher I remember reading Alfie Kohn's (1999) book *Punished by Rewards: The Trouble With Gold Stars, Incentive Plans, A's, Praise, and Other*

Bribes and loving the voice (and sense) of the author. He tells the tale of a conversation with educational psychologist John Nicholls about the effectiveness of reading incentive programs. Nicholls evidently suggested that by having incentive programs sponsored by fast food restaurants, we are not creating young people who love to read but instead are creating young people who love to eat. Kohn (1999) extended Nicholls' quip to the danger of all incentives tied to academic achievement—even grades (*gasp*). His book goes into great detail about how we should be motivating our students. (*Spoiler alert*: He suggests we focus on collaboration, content, and choice in the classroom.)

I want to take this a bit further, though. I was a teacher who focused on Kohn's (1999) three C's of motivation, but there were still students I couldn't reach. You see, motivation is tricky and there are a gazillion variables that can influence a student's behavior in your class at any given moment. Although we can't control many of those variables, we can understand them.

Goal orientation is one of those variables that affects motivation. You can think of goal orientation as how you feel about challenges and how you define success—the interaction of your feeling with your definition influences how you approach or avoid goals. It sounds more complicated than it is.

> You can think of goal orientation
> as how you feel about challenges
> and how you define success.

Imagine that your dad drops you off at a new school for summer volleyball tryouts. You've never been very athletic, but he thinks this could be your thing. Because he's your dad, you believe him. So, you walk into the gym determined to do your best and to release your hidden volleyball talents. At this point, you are focused on being successful and making the team. How does the coach motivate you? She probably corrects your form, coaches you to put more power into your serves, and gives little positive reinforcement. The coach is looking for the best players for her team and wants to see if you have what it takes.

After some time, you realize that you (sadly) have no hidden volleyball talent and your primary focus shifts to avoiding failure. You don't want to break any bones, and you don't want to embarrass yourself. How does the coach motivate you now? She likely partners you with someone of similar ability, coaches you on one skill at a time, and praises you on your positive attitude. The coach wants to ensure that everyone who tries out for the team learns something about the game and, whether you make the team or not, you feel good about being there and taking a risk.

We want our students to approach their goals with the desire to achieve success, not just to avoid failure.

Don't we have both types of students in our classes? Those who want to be the best and those who want to survive? Consider these two beliefs about goals. Some people set goals focused on achieving something; this achievement is equated to their success. Others set goals that are focused on avoiding failure. Knowing what you know about grit and mindset, which do you think we want to encourage in our students? We want our students to approach their goals with the desire to achieve success, not just to avoid failure. But, as you recall from the volleyball scenarios, they don't all come to us this way. We, like the coach, need to recognize that these differences exist so that we can effectively motivate every student.

Another component to understand is that students can have a mastery orientation or a performance orientation that affects how they view success and failure. A student with mastery orientation defines success by comparing herself to her prior performances. She has a solid understanding of her skills and focuses on improvement. A student with performance orientation defines success by comparing herself to others' achievements. She wants the superlative—the most creative idea, the fastest mile time, etc.

The distinction between orientations is tricky because my brain wants to compartmentalize these into positive and negative behaviors. I lean toward the belief that mastery orientation is "better" than performance orientation because it is focused on self-growth, but it's not so clear-cut.

A person with performance orientation thrives in competitive environments and believes she is in control of her success. Those are positive qualities in certain settings. A person with mastery orientation may not reach her full potential because she is measuring success on her prior achievements. That's not so positive because she may be limiting herself. The other thing to keep in mind, as if we need to make this even trickier, is that a person doesn't identify with one orientation all of the time in all areas. In fact, it is better to think of these as continuums that constantly evolve. Table 3 shows how mastery and performance orientation can manifest in students, and Table 4 shows ways in which to support students with either orientation.

So, what do you do? You get to know your students. This is the part of your job that will require the greatest amount of effort, but pays the highest reward. If your students and their parents truly believe that you care about them, they will work that much harder for you. So, as soon as you walk through the doors of your school, you put on your teacher face and get it done. You greet your students at your classroom door with eye contact, a smile, and, a hug, a high five, or a handshake.

When there is downtime, you find out your students' interests and make connections with them. If Jimmy is into Pokémon, well you message your high school friend who is always posting about Pikachu on Facebook to find out what to say to Jimmy. Jimmy doesn't care if you know what you're talking about or not—he may

TABLE 3

Mastery Orientation and Performance Orientation in Students

Mastery Orientation	Performance Orientation
• Anastasia reads voraciously, especially historical fiction. • Marc's teachers describe him as happy and a hard worker. • Georgia doesn't really care about her grades and often leaves her graded work behind in the classroom. • Elaina resists assignments that she thinks are too easy and may complain or refuse to do them. • Carl loves to talk through math story problems and generate creative solutions.	• Jen pursues academic competitions on the weekends. • Bobby's teachers describe him as a rule follower and a good student. • Lauren is eager to see her grades, but often cries when they're lower than an "A." • Frank can memorize facts, but struggles when asked to demonstrate deep understanding. • Tatiana loves adding her stickers to the math chart in the classroom and often makes a big deal about it.

TABLE 4

How to Support Students With Mastery Orientation and Performance Orientation

Supporting a Student With Mastery Orientation	Supporting a Student With Performance Orientation
Reward the behaviors you want students to repeat: • striving for academic excellence, and • viewing academic competition as healthy.	Reward the behaviors you want students to repeat: • academic risk-taking, • positive support of peers, and • self-discipline.

look at you like you're beneath him (and, in Pokémon world you just might be), but he will appreciate that you cared enough to try.

If you can, pop by one of your students' music performances, sporting events, or religious ceremonies—they will love you forever. If you can't, ask for pictures of them doing their thing so you can create a bulletin board in the classroom. Laugh, and be silly when you can. (I should tell you here that I'm not a naturally silly person. I'm very introverted, so I found I could be silliest when I was around my goofy teacher friends. They helped pull me out of my shell.) Celebrate your students' birthdays and other meaningful moments. Remember that you—yes, you—may be the only one to care. "I see you" is a powerful message, and, for many of us, it's all that we want—to be seen.

This is all part of honing your craft. Sure, you're a teacher who is an expert in one or more content areas, but you're also an expert in children. You cultivate a community of learners who value the experience and you recognize that their needs are as unique as they are. You design lessons that require your students to take risks and you push them to find their passions. And you go to bed every night knowing that you're doing your absolute best.

Final Thoughts

I've failed over and over and over again in my life. And that is why I succeed.

—Michael Jordan

Intrinsically, we know the power of having a positive mindset. As teachers, we've seen students kick it into gear after a little pep talk. But now, we also have research and science to support our work in helping our students believe in themselves. The tightrope you walk every day is being the one who encourages every student, without becoming the one they rely on for validation. We can use our understanding of mastery and performance orientation

---

Fixed Mindset ◄ - - - - - - - - - - - - - ► Growth Mindset

FIGURE 7. *Growth mindset continuum.*

---

to shape how we motivate our students and help us understand where they are coming from in times of frustration. Finally, we need to commit to making hard work a habit. Set the bar high and your students will meet you there. #promise

Discussion Questions

1. Evaluate the culture of your school in terms of the overarching mindset. Where do you fall in the continuum (see Figure 7) and what does this mean for your students and staff?

2. Consider Kohn's (1999) recommendation that we motivate students by focusing on collaboration, content, and choice. In which of these three areas can you focus on improving and how can you do this?

3. Think about the growth and fixed mindset. Describe the students you have that fit into each category and discuss how you approach and motivate each student.

Chapter 5

Cultivating Passionate Students

I was at dinner with some friends a few years ago and one friend asked us all to name three of our passions. Three?!? I had so many that I just couldn't decide which three were so important that I would tell this group. My fervor for my passions changed often and here I was, at dinner, going to be forever memorialized by these three things. It's possible that I was the only one panicking. But then, talking later, I found out that some of my friends struggled to come up with three. They maybe had one or two objects of passion, but not three. Hmmm. Passion is such an elusive and provocative topic because everyone can be an "expert" while no one really knows anything. I do know this: Passion is a critical component of grit. It's the ultimate "why" that is too important to ignore. This chapter will explore ideas for cultivating passion in students in an era of standardized testing and school funding issues.

Take a moment to think of something you've worked hard to achieve, something that required a certain amount of passion to

DOI: 10.4324/9781003235385-5

maintain focus. You may describe this achievement like Leonard Cohen described writing lyrics: "It is a mysterious process, it involves perseverance and perspiration and sometimes, by some grace, something stands out and invites you to elaborate or animate it" (as cited in Boyd, 2016, para. 2). The thing is, passion *is* mysterious and can definitely be difficult to articulate. But I'm going to try . . .

Passion is a critical component of grit. It's the ultimate "why" that is too important to ignore.

When asked further about his creative process, Cohen indicated a reluctance to go into much detail. He said, "These are sacred mechanics and you have to be careful analyzing them as you would never write a line again. If you looked too deeply into the process you'd end up in a state of paralysis" (as cited in Boyd, 2016, para. 2). It reminds me of the poem by Billy Collins (1996) in which he describes readers (perhaps teachers?) beating a poem with a hose just to figure out what it means. Cohen and Collins touched on the same idea, that passion is enigmatic and wonderful. So let's think about what it means to cultivate passionate students without ending up paralyzed or beaten.

But first, let's talk about the elephant in your classroom. State testing. Lack of funding. (Okay, two elephants. And not the cute kind, either.) I get it. You have so much on your plate. Maybe your salary is dependent on your students' performance on standardized assessments. Or maybe you don't even have the materials to teach your content, let alone "cultivate passion." Maybe you don't feel like you have the autonomy to make curriculum decisions.

Aren't you exhausted? Aren't you burned out by the paperwork and accountability and lack of appreciation and . . . ? Don't you sometimes wonder how much longer you can do this? Or if all of "this" is worth it? First of all, cultivating passion in your students is the way to get back to why you started. Passionate people are lively and engaged. Those are fun people to be around. But there's more . . .

Chris Hadfield is a retired Canadian astronaut and is a really fascinating guy. Sure, he's been to space a couple of times, but he's also a social media superstar, writer, comedian, and musician. Seriously, look him up. He's clearly no stranger to passion. When he was in space, he communicated on Reddit with his followers. From space. (No more excuses as to why your inbox is full.) Hadfield is noted for his advice to youngsters:

> Every decision you make, from what you eat to what you do with your time tonight, turns you into who you are tomorrow, and the day after that. Look at who you want to be, and start sculpting yourself into that person. . . . Don't let life randomly kick you into the adult you don't want to become (as cited in Kantrowitz, 2013, para. 8).

Hadfield encouraged his followers to be intentional with their choices and to pursue interests that get them closer to their dreams. He also recognized that we can decide who we want to be and that we, ultimately, are responsible for who we become. Isn't that excellent advice? Haven't you been telling your students this very thing since the first day of school? I know you have, but here's the thing: Hadfield's guidance stems from personal interest and passion and that makes all the difference. I think we can do this very same thing in our classrooms, in spite of the elephants. By purposefully cultivating passion in our students, we can bring the fun back *and* get on with our mission to raise them to be responsible and gritty human beings.

Don't follow your passion. Yes, you read that correctly.

Notice that the verb in the title of this chapter is "cultivate." It's not "find" or "follow," and Cal Newport, Georgetown professor and author, explains why this is important in his 2012 CNN article "Why 'Follow your Passion' Is Bad Advice." Essentially, Newport argued that passion is not something you one day wake up to or something that hits you like a lightning strike.

First, Newport (2012) suggested that people who enjoy their jobs, who in turn describe themselves as being passionate about their careers, are afforded competence, respect, autonomy, creativity, and sense of impact. Their "passion" comes from experiencing each of these regularly and authentically. So let's talk about how these attributes can be emphasized in your classes.

Competence

It's in our nature to want to feel "good enough." Whether that's referring to being good enough for our partner, our job, our kids. . . . We don't want to feel like failures and our students are just like us. I know—crazy. It's important to provide students with opportunities to feel genuinely successful and to regularly feel competent.

I recently worked with someone with much more experience than me. She was a great writer with a vision for what our job entailed (as opposed to me, who was figuring things out along the way). Although this was an excellent opportunity for me to learn from the best, it didn't exactly work out that way. Everything I wrote and submitted to her for approval was ripped to pieces. She would call me in regularly to painstakingly go over her suggestions for how I could improve my writing. Essentially, she changed my words into hers. Although I believe I had much to learn from her, I had also been around long enough to know that writing style is subjective and she was crossing over from teacher to word slayer. Within a few months, I was unable to see past my overwhelming feeling of incompetence in order to learn from her. Instead, I would get called into her office, gird my loins, and endure the killing of my words and confidence. I was miserable. And, you guessed it, misery is not ideal for cultivating passion.

> Create learning experiences designed to lead your students to feeling competent.

Do you remember Vygotsgy's (Daniels, 2005) Zone of Proximal Development? (Quick review: ZPD is what we now think of as scaffolding. You design learning experiences just beyond what a student can do alone, but provide the support necessary to achieve success. The zone continues to move as the child's skills develop.) Consider this zone as you design your lessons and focus on developing competency of that lesson's objective. The first step is to figure out what your students know. You can do this by having students describe what they know about a topic or you can give them a more formal preassessment. This process should be focused on the main objective of the lesson, not on the details. Essentially, consider what you want your students to remember about the lesson 10 years from now—that should be at the center of your assessment of what they know.

Most importantly, create learning experiences designed to lead your students to feeling competent. This doesn't mean that you hand out a trophy when your students master the objective or that you dilute your content; it just means that you are making room for all students to be and feel competent in your classroom.

Respect and Autonomy

Creating a culture of respect begins the first day of class. Sure, you're the ultimate boss, but you also need to show that you value your students and their opinions. You respect them as human beings and accept that they may not love your class or your content or you as much as you would like (#thetruthhurts).

We must also create classrooms for our students that center on autonomy, responsibility, and self-control. On the surface, these may not seem directly linked to passion, but consider Bob Dylan trying to cultivate passion in an environment that allowed for no independence, where he was painfully micromanaged by his producers. Or Julia Child mastering French cuisine under the tutelage of an overbearing mentor. Passion is closely tied to joy and it's nearly impossible to experience joy when you feel oppressed.

Give students choices.

Obviously autonomy looks different depending on the age of your students, but it's so very important to find little ways to hand some of the power over. I tried this in a variety of ways over the years. Some attempts were more successful than others, depending on the particular kids I was working with. I rarely had a seating chart and counted on students to make good choices in where they chose to sit. One year I had a sign out sheet to use the restroom—instead of students having to ask me for permission, they took the pass and signed themselves out and then back in.

I was most effective at curriculum differentiation when I structured my classes within the blended learning framework. Blended learning is the combination of face-to-face and online instruction. It requires a great deal of front-loading and planning of activities (and technology, obviously), but it's a sparkly kind of magic when students are in control of their learning.

I almost always gave students choice in the order of their assignments. If they wanted to work on their writing in class, but they're reading at home, that was okay with me as long as they came prepared for our discussion. I gave them choice in the difficulty of their assignments. I told them up front which was the hardest and then they could pick. (More often than not the students who struggled in school chose the hardest option—they were just itching to be successful and to prove they were smart. You can bet that I worked closely with them to make that happen.) You get the idea. Give students choices.

Creativity

When we are given autonomy and respect, we have the freedom to be creative. We can come up with new ways to solve problems and new problems to solve. So just by making small adjustments in your classroom's balance of power, you are already providing your students with the space needed to be creative.

Like the other tenets of a passion-building environment, creativity should be infused into your curriculum and not just tacked on at the end as an extension activity. It's also not breaking out the markers and feathers. It's offering open-ended responses and choice in how a student can demonstrate mastery of a concept.

> Creativity should be infused into your curriculum and not just tacked on at the end as an extension activity.

Creativity is also divergent thinking. Give students a problem—this problem could be mathematical, historical, scientific, artistic, grammatical, musical, etc.—and have them generate as many possible ways to solve that problem. This forces students, to use a trite phrase, to "think outside the box." I also love the idea of the 100 Day Project (Luna & The Great Discontent, 2017). Students choose to create something (anything) and do that for 100 days. They could write a lyric to a song, make up a new dance, take a photograph, etc., every day for 100 days. Depending on their experience with their chosen medium, they will have to be creative in order to maintain the originality over 100 days.

Sense of Impact

This is my favorite of Newport's (2012) attributes. You can kindle the passion of your students by helping them see that their actions and their learning matter. "Authentic assessment" is more than a buzzword. It's a reality of effective lesson design and it's not going away.

Help students see that their actions
and their learning matter.

If we're going to be honest, we know that everything we do does not have a great impact on humanity. Authentic assessments begin with an essential question—these questions provide the guiding purpose for your lessons and they get to the significance. Even though you're teaching a lesson on fractions, you're actually helping students understand how many parts create a whole and that each part is important. It's not a big leap to understanding that they are those parts that create your whole classroom/school/team. Ultimately the authentic assessment, the culminating activity, should be engaging and directly tied to the essential question. By designing these learning experiences for your students, you are providing them with the path between the "Why do we have to know this" and the "Ahhhh, I get it now" moment.

Design Thinking: A New Wave
of Authentic Assessment

Design thinking is one of the more recent spins on authentic assessment. IDEO (2017) breaks it down into four phases: (1) gather inspiration by studying what people need, (2) generate ideas beyond the obvious solutions, (3) make ideas tangible by building prototypes, and (4) sharing the results to spur others into action. Design thinking is similar to problem-based learning; however, rather than beginning with a problem to solve or question to answer, design thinking is rooted in empathy. You may be thinking there isn't much difference between the two, but there is. And that difference is the focus on the people the product will affect. Think of it like a web with the issue in the center and a brainstorm of ways this issue could affect the people involved surrounding it.

Just for a moment think about your students who cut in line, who cheat, who struggle with compromise. By regularly incorporating empathy into your lessons, we can address social and emotional issues authentically as opposed to creating singular lessons on trust, respect, or a number of other character values.

As a teacher, you are essential to this process, but it involves some magic. That is, you need to lead students to the answers, but you can't give them the answers. The magic is knowing the kinds of questions to ask. For example, Karen is studying the Amazon rainforest, which is a pretty big topic. Karen and her teacher talk, and Karen reveals that she chose this topic because she loves river otters, but they are in danger because of the illegal logging. Her teacher asks the following questions. If Karen knows the answers, she adds them to her web. If she doesn't, she adds them to her list of research questions.

- Why are people logging in the Amazon?
- What is the difference between legal and illegal logging in the Amazon?
- Why is it so important to log the Amazonian timber?
- What happens to the people who illegally log in the Amazon?

The answers to these questions lead to more questions until your students can really get to the issues that relate to people, tapping into the empathy that is so important to this process.

The second step of design thinking involves organizing and prioritizing information regarding the topic. This is an exercise in critical thinking. First, students gather all available information on their topic and then they prioritize it based on credibility and relevance. This is where teachers provide lessons on propaganda and evaluating sources, specifically addressing issues that arise through Internet research. In order to prioritize the information, students must firmly understand the issue and they must work together to remain focused on what is most important.

Design thinking is a strategic process for cultivating passion in students.

The first two steps of design thinking typically pique students' interests and build the passion necessary for the third step: generating ideas. The generation of ideas may be the most reliable representations of creativity. Think about it. I've stared into the blank eyes of a student who could not generate an idea no matter how I prodded him. And then I've had to interrupt another student who just wouldn't stop talking. There was an absolute and very clear difference in each student's ability to generate ideas. This step is a focused brainstorming process that involves funneling the research into a product that can address the issue.

Finally, it is time to follow through by creating a product that is helpful to the people involved. This is where students get hung up and often don't complete the design thinking process. By now, they have spent a significant amount of time and energy thinking about the issue and it takes a certain amount of perseverance to maintain focus and bring it home.

Essentially, design thinking is a strategic process for cultivating passion in students. You introduce a problem to your students in order to incite their curiosity as they tackle how this problem affects others, conduct research, and offer a potential solution. When done well (which isn't easy, by the way), you have created opportunities for your students to open their eyes to new issues, built their empathetic capacity, and strengthened their problem-solving skills.

Content Standards and Passion: An Oxymoron?

At best, you might be thinking that I'm making some sense. At worst, you're thinking I'm somewhere between a looney tune and an out-of-touch member of the ivory tower. Don't give up on me yet. I know you're thinking that all of this passion business sounds good, but what about the standards? The tests? The evaluations? The competency-based pay? The good news is that this is not an either-or situation. Think of it more as an all-in situation. Let's take a look at some standards . . .

> Texas Essential Knowledge and Skills for Social Studies, Kindergarten, 10(D): Use voting as a method for group decision making. (Texas Education Agency, 2011)

Now think about everything you can do with that. It not only ties in to autonomy, but is open-ended enough that students can surely apply this to an area of passion. What do kindergarten students love? Free time, stickers, puppies, snacks . . .

> Ohio's Learning Standards for Mathematics, Grade 6, Critical Area 1: Connecting ratio and rate to whole number multiplication and division and using concepts of ratio and rate to solve problems. (Ohio Department of Education, 2017)

Again, although this standard is specific to a focused skill, it's broad enough that it can be applied to any area. The key to authentically allowing students to connect a standard like this to their passions is cross-curricular lessons. Remember that you don't need to have all of the answers. If you know that your students are working on a persuasive research project in language arts, ask them to create a way that they can demonstrate the concepts of rate and ratio related to that project. The beauty here (and lean in because I'm whispering this secret to you) is that your students are actually creating their lesson. Your job is to make sure they understand rate and ratio, offer small-group instruction when necessary, and evaluate their applications of these skills. Bam. Passion collides with content.

Next Generation Science Standards for California Public Schools: HS-LS1-1. Construct an explanation based on evidence for how the structure of DNA determines the structure of proteins which carry out the essential functions of life through systems of specialized cells. (California Department of Education, 2015)

That's a doozy of a standard. Clearly, it's very specific and it's not easy to ask students to connect this to their interests. So this is what you do: You get to the heart of the "so what" behind the content. Honestly, I haven't thought about DNA in 25 years and I'm doing okay. Depending on the directions your students are heading, they may or may not care about DNA after they leave your classroom. But, do they care about genetics and what they've inherited from their biological parents on a cellular level? Have they thought about their personality traits and how they behave similarly/differently from their family members? Is their behavior inherited or learned? Very few teenagers grow up wanting to be like their parents, but how much control do we really have? *That* is something high school students care about. By sharing the "so what" of the lesson, you've connected the content to them, which is fundamental to building interest and passion.

Back to Basics: What Is Passion?

Research on passion is often tied to productivity and entrepreneurship. Take a look at the following definitions of passion:
- "Passion is the energy that can fuel a project or a task" (Kaufman, as cited in frog, 2012).
- Passion is a genuine love of work and measured in "emotions of love, attachment, and longing" (Baum & Locke, 2004, p. 588).
- Passion is "emotional energy, drive, and spirit" (Bird, 1989, p. 8).

If you're like me, you're viewing those definitions and thinking, "Yeah, I know that feeling. But how in the world am I going to get my students to feel that? I mean, I can't even get them to _____ (tie their shoes; turn in their homework; come to class; fill in the blank)." Lucky for you (and for me), some people have come up with some great ideas to help us figure them out.

Passion building begins early.

When you talk with passionate adults, they will tell you that their interests began in childhood. So, this means that play and experimentation are super important in elementary school. This means that teachers must prioritize exploration and investigation. Not only must early elementary classes be places of passion building, but we can't lose focus when students move on to middle and high school. Sure, things become more "serious" but (as I'm sure you're figuring out) cultivating passion is serious business.

Kaufman (as cited in frog, 2012), like Cal Newport (2012), also suggested that passion stems from feelings of self-efficacy. You should realize by now that passion is a jumbled crossing of wires: interest, ability, time, resources, commitment. . . . It's impossible to figure out where passion starts and ends because all of the components operate simultaneously. If you're a linear person, this might drive you crazy. But think of this: You can select any component of passion and build a nexus of intensity from there. So let's talk about how these components can be emphasized in your classes.

- **Interest.** Create open learning experiences so students can select their own topics. Design opportunities for students to explore their interests and to reflect on how these have changed over time.
- **Ability.** Focus on your students' strengths and encourage them to investigate those. Help them find extensions from their skills to future areas of study.
- **Time.** Decide what you can abandon in favor of cultivating passion. You may have to let go of something you are passionate about in order to make time for your students. (I know. They take and take and take.)

- **Resources.** Explore crowdfunding options (e.g., Donors Choose.org, AdoptAClassroom.org, and GoFundMe). Write grants. Ask for donations. Teachers are the most resourceful people I know, so just keep doing what you've always been doing.
- **Commitment.** Require commitment from your students. Obviously this varies based on the age of your students, but lessons designed to cultivate passion should also build their capacity to persevere through challenges and maintain focus.

So now let's talk about how you can take these ideas and create a culture conducive to cultivating passion.

Make your classroom a place where it's cool, welcomed, and required to be passionate.

Passionate people can seem a little crazy at times. And your typical middle and high school student wants to stay far from being labeled in that way. You know what that means, right? You, the leader of your classroom, need to make crazy the new normal. Be crazy for art or history fun facts or complicated equations. Don't be afraid to completely geek out in front of your students.

Make your classroom a place where it's cool, welcomed, and required to be passionate. When I taught eighth grade, it was easy to recognize the passions of some of my students because they weren't afraid to go all in. I had students who wrote obsessively about their favorite bands or only read nonfiction about the environment. Their existence revolved around their passions, so I would have had to be completely obtuse not to recognize them. But, looking back, I couldn't tell you what some of the others were really into. They didn't wear their passions on their sleeves. Sure, I knew the kind of books they liked to read and some of their interests, but I didn't know what they would give it up all for. It's possible that they didn't even have "a thing." Again, that's where I could have done better. Remember all of those ideas for establishing rapport with your students? Do those.

You should also know that I'm an introvert. I don't enjoy staff development where I have to make a skit or perform interpretive dance or anything like that. I would rather discuss important issues in a small group than create and present a poster about the new discipline policy. So being a crazy person and nerding out in front of judgmental 14-year-olds is not my idea of a good time. Except that we're talking about my passion. I have no fear of being "all in" when it comes to great books or influential writers or research on grit. Why? Because I genuinely am crazy about those things. I admire the teachers who dance and sing with their students, but that's just not me. The bottom line is this: You do you—just do it with passion.

Final Thoughts

> Nothing is as important as passion. No matter what you want to do with your life, be passionate.
>
> —Jon Bon Jovi

Cultivating passion is an everyday endeavor. It should be subtly infused throughout your lessons and discussed often. Competence, respect, autonomy, creativity, sense of impact. Imagine if you committed to incorporating those five tenets of passion into your curriculum, if every day you and your students were tackling the content in ways that aligned with building passion. The electricity in your room would be palpable—you and your students would be learning and having fun, the perfect environment for building passion.

Discussion Questions

1. How do you cultivate passion in your class(es)?
2. Newport (2012) suggested that passion can be built in an environment focused on competence, respect, autonomy, creativity, and sense of impact. Of these, which do you do well and where can you improve? Map out steps you can take.
3. Within your curriculum standards, where can you authentically incorporate design thinking? Brainstorm ideas for projects and building empathy.

Chapter 6

Building Grit at Home

Before I begin this chapter, can we just agree that parenting is the best and hardest thing in the world? I vacillate between feeling like a rockstar and a complete failure. Some days I wake up, whip up a batch of instant oatmeal, and kiss my kids on their heads while I head out to work, feeling like there should be awards for moms like me. And other days (well, most days), I feel like I'm not doing enough, doing too much, not strict enough, too strict. . . . Basically, I'm just a few dichotomies away from never getting out of bed (#whoswithme).

Good news! Grit *can* be strategically developed through failure and healthy responses. The most efficient way to do this is by combining efforts between school and home. This chapter will provide ideas for how you can educate your students' parents on the importance of developing grit, even if it isn't always fun.

Parents need to consider the three components of grit (passion, perseverance, and commitment).

DOI: 10.4324/9781003235385-6

As a teacher, you've committed yourself to furthering the well-being of your students, but guess what? Those students have parents, so it's kind of a package deal. As much as you want to design your lessons to build your students' grit, you need to realize that this is a team effort that requires buy-in from everyone involved. Parenting a child with grit in mind is really very simple. Parents need to consider the three components of grit (passion, perseverance, and commitment) and then determine how they can build their children's capacity for each of these. It could get ugly and it won't always be easy, but it can be done.

From the first day of school, you need to communicate to parents that you genuinely care for their children, that you would do anything for them, and that you are an advocate for their needs. When parents believe that you come from a place of love and grace, they are more willing to support you. And you're going to need that support, because building a child's capacity for grit can be a bit of a mess.

Parenting Styles

Parenting has the greatest influence on the development of children than any other factor (Baumrind, 1966). Read that again and tell me if your chest doesn't constrict a little. Sure, you are an essential person in your students' lives, but in most cases you fall behind the parents in terms of influence. There are three parenting styles that are pretty widely accepted among developmental psychologists: permissive, authoritarian, and authoritative (Baumrind, 1966).

The permissive parenting style is exactly what it sounds like: The parent is not an authority in the child's life. This can take on different forms depending on the family dynamic. One parent can consult with the child regarding expectations and rules, almost treating the relationship as a partnership. Another parent may just be uninvolved in the child's life and, by default, allows the child to make her own decisions. I know my kids would love this style, especially my teenage daughter who is convinced that I am the most embarrassing/lame/strict mother on the planet. As teachers, I bet you are picturing the kids in your class whose parents have adopted this style. They're easy to spot, right? They likely don't follow your rules or respect their peers. When they're challenged, they give up. And they may also have difficulty making and keeping friends because of these behaviors. Of course there are outliers, but the typical child with permissive parents will not grow up to be gritty.

The authoritarian parenting style is essentially the opposite of permissive. The parent exercises absolute power and truly believes that obedience is a virtue. Order and structure are important facets of the household, and rules and expectations are not negotiable. The child is punished if the rules are not followed. Although children who are parented in this style often perform well in school, they can also grow into anxious and unhappy individuals. They do not know how to cope with frustration and either lash out or give up. Remember that grit is built from circumstances that allow a child to persevere through challenges; a child with authoritarian parents is not given these opportunities and will likely not develop grit.

> Children with authoritative parents are socially adjusted and can typically face challenges with confidence.

Obviously I'm leading up to the parenting style that has the most positive impact on child development: authoritative. An authoritative parent is somewhere in the middle of permissive and authoritarian. This parent makes rules, sets expectations, and uses reason to explain the decisions made. Although the parent exerts power, it is not absolute. Children with authoritative parents are socially adjusted and can typically face challenges with confidence.

Not only is authoritative parenting supported by research as *the* recommended style by child psychologists, Duckworth (2016) also found that this balance of being demanding and supportive led to children growing up grittier. Essentially, her research highlighted the importance of parents knowing their children, their capabilities, and what they want for themselves. Being a parent of gritty children involves balancing this information so that parents know how to respond when their child is struggling or wants to give up.

Although you can't control the parenting styles of the parents of your students, you can understand how to best work with all types of parents. Keep in mind that no one wants to be told how to parent; however, parents do typically want the best for their children and in this changing world may not know how. Again, approach parents with an attitude of teamwork and a focus on helping their children develop into healthy, independent adults.

> Although you can't control the parenting
> styles of the parents of your students,
> you can understand how to best
> work with all types of parents.

As early as you can into the school year, teach your parents about the components of grit and give them concrete ideas for how they can support your efforts at home. Throughout the year, continue to emphasize the importance of this skill so that parents internalize the language and use it with their children. Parents will understand the need for their children to have interests that they pursue persistently. It's not a difficult concept to grasp. However, they may need your support in understanding what they can do to further this pursuit.

In the ideal world, you would have this conversation face-to-face with parents. Or, better yet, your students would have the talk with their parents. However, if all else fails, you can address grit in your syllabus or parent letter just to make sure everyone is on the same page. Figure 8 is an example of a letter you can send to parents to discuss grit.

Parenting Suggestions for Building Grit

Grit is the result of persistence and passion. Grit cannot be cultivated in an environment where children are given everything they want. It also can't be developed if they never get a taste of earned success. That's the bottom line and really all you need to know. But, for those of you who love lists and concrete advice, here you go.

It Takes a Village

Because there are limits to what we are capable of as humans and there are also limits to how much our children will believe us, it is important for parents to engage their children in activities beyond school. Grit is like a muscle. You need a bit of it to begin with and then, as you work it out, you become grittier and grittier. Your max-out moment increases as your grit grows.

Duckworth (2016) suggested that parents involve their children in extracurricular activities. The reasons behind this are plenty. Parents are:

1. sending the message that they support their children's interests,
2. helping children find and/or deepen an interest,
3. giving children opportunities to practice perseverance, and
4. expanding children's capacity to be gritty.

Dear parents,

I am so excited about this year and have so many wonderful lessons planned for your child! I am going to challenge and excite my students like never before—my classroom will be a magical place of wonder, authentic learning, and *grit*. However, in order to pull this off, I need your help.

The key to making sure your child is fully prepared for next year is high expectations. Like a baseball player at training camp, I am going to push your child to write at a quality he or she has never written at before. We're going to practice, practice, practice. It's going to get messy and it may not be pretty because—let's face it—hard work is often not fun.

Here is what I need from you: Support your child and remind him or her that this is possible. Hard work really does pay off. If your child says that my class is too hard (and you will likely hear this), emphasize all of the growth that will happen. Connect this hard work to the commitment and perseverance of your child's idol.

Here is what you will get: A gritty kid who knows what it's like to face obstacles and overcome them. You will also get a child who believes in the importance of hard work and, even more important, believes in him- or herself. You will get a child who is passionate about learning and can articulate his or her interests and strengths as a learner.

I hope you are in this with me. Together we can make this the best year ever! I genuinely appreciate your support.

Sincerely,
Laila Sanguras

FIGURE 8. *Sample parent letter introducing grit.*

She also suggested that when children reach high school, parents should require a one-year commitment from their children regarding extracurricular activities. It's at this point that the interest is expanding to include nuances that will be missed if a child is allowed to flit from activity to activity. Hopefully all of the flitting was done in the early years.

Parents can't do this alone, however. They need coaches, mentors, and magic makers. By allowing their children to work with another adult, a coach-like figure, the responsibility of building grit is taken off of their shoulders a bit.

There is a wondrous window when kids believe their parents know everything. As small children, they look to us with big eyes and just take in all of our wisdom. They will defend what we say to their siblings and playground bullies. But then when you aren't looking, the window is slammed shut and you're the lamest human on the planet. *This* is why we need to involve our children in extracurricular activities. As our kids grow up, they've come to realize there are limitations to our knowledge.

My son used to ask me about how he was doing at his baseball games and I would typically praise him. Sometimes I would comment on how he could have stolen a base or something, but couldn't really support my comments with any facts. Although he still loves me, he recognizes that I've hit the ceiling on my baseball knowledge and now he goes to my husband, who can remember every single play and explain where he made smart decisions and where he could have been more of a risk taker. As my son's interest and skills increase, he needs more guidance. If he sticks with me, he won't improve and he certainly won't be grittier. He needs something more and it's my responsibility to help him find that.

Teach Children to Honor Their Commitments

I read a parenting magazine when I was pregnant with my first child (and had the time to read magazines), and I remember the author's clear advice: When kids ask for something, whether the parent says yes or no, mean it. There is no place in parenting (or teaching) for a waffler, especially if we want to build grit in children. Children need to know that parents listen and believe them when they say they want something. They also need to know that when their parents make a rule, set an expectation, or say no that they mean it and no amount of begging/crying/rolling on the floor will change that.

> ## Encourage the parents of your students to talk with their children about their own commitments and the struggles they've faced when honoring them.

A person cannot develop grit without commitment; otherwise, you just quit when something gets hard or when your interest wanes. Encourage the parents of your students to talk with their children about their own commitments and the struggles they've faced when honoring them. First of all, kids emulate their parents. They also want to know that their parents are human. As part of the learning/teaching process about what it means to be gritty, encourage your students' parents to talk with their kids about times they wanted to quit something and didn't, or a time they did quit and how that felt. Parents often feel that they have to set the perfect example for their children, but because grit can be so messy and painful to develop, kids are better off if they have a sense of what this looks like in reality. They also need to understand that even adults experience the same feelings they do.

However, parents also need to be demanding about the right things at the right time. No one is perfect, right? We are all struggling with something. Kids are, too. Although parents should encourage their children to honor their commitments, they also need to know when to lighten up and give their kids a break. I wish I could provide you with an "if, then" flowchart that you could distribute on the first day of school, but this is where their expertise as parents comes in. As a teacher, you can help reassure parents of this. I don't know one parent who wouldn't benefit from a little encouragement, some positive feedback, and a reminder that we can do this.

Help Children Find Themselves

Remember that grit is built in passionate environments, but that it's impossible to become truly passionate about something unless you're immersed in it. Well, a child is incapable of doing that alone and needs a parent's support. Parents need to encourage their kids to find their "thing" and to pursue it. One of my little boys loved trains from a very early age. His love went beyond the average Thomas the Tank Engine interest; he loved trains and would watch countless videos, look at picture books, and talk about trains. He was captivated and couldn't believe the rest of us were bored to tears. Well, when he turned 5, we put him in soccer just as we had with his older brothers. He was minimally invested and showed little interest in the game. But, being the youngest of six, he wanted an identity, so he would proudly tell people that he was a soccer player. This year we put him in a robotics course where he works in a lab every Monday night writing code and running experiments. He's 7. He *loves* robotics class and will forego just about anything to get back into the lab. After two slightly excruciating soccer seasons, we are all thrilled that he now confidently describes himself as an engineer. (And we're out of the snack-duty rotation. Hallelujah.)

Kids should be allowed to be bored.
Part of finding yourself is figuring out
what to do when you have free time.

Every child needs a passion, a "go-to" activity when there is downtime. As you know, children's interests change rapidly and often without notice, but children's interests are limited to their experiences. For instance, my little engineer would never even know it was possible for him to program a robot unless we had enrolled him in this course. It's why, when you ask children what they want to be when they grow up, they suggest what they know: teacher, firefighter, bird . . .

But, a super important part of this is that, although parents are integral in exposing their children to a variety of experiences, you are *not*, as my mother used to say, the entertainment coordinator. Kids should be allowed to be bored. Part of finding yourself is figuring out what to do when you have free time. Part of establishing an identity is being in charge of that free time. Having that choice is empowering, especially as a child. As an adult, are you ever bored? I'm not. I relish my downtime when I can choose to do anything I want to do. Children should get to experience that, too.

You Work Hard, They Work Hard

Parents are their child's first teacher, so children will learn what it means to "work hard" from their parents. You can help facilitate that by working with children to set goals for themselves and discussing these goals with their parents. As a unit, everyone becomes aware of what it means to work toward something and then everyone can celebrate the successes along the way. Undoubtedly, circumstances will arise that a child needs to work out of, which is exactly what is needed to build the grit to successfully endure even more difficult situations.

Prepare your parents. Tell them that their child will struggle, but that it's worth it.

You also need to be sure parents understand that, while building grit is essential to raising independent and successful adults, it's hard. As a teacher, you design learning experiences to challenge your students and you scaffold those assignments to allow the students to be successful. But when a kid is 7 and wants to go to recess, or 13 and wants to talk to her friends, or 17 and has to go to work, she doesn't want to work hard. She wants to move on with "good enough" effort that really is far from good enough. Prepare your parents for this. Tell them that their child will struggle, but that it's worth it. Tell them that their child will want to quit, but you'll be there every step of the way. Parents need to understand that this is coming so they can prepare themselves and can support their children at home.

It's also helpful to discuss how parents should praise their children, focusing on the process of learning, struggling, and persevering. Although it's easy to celebrate the A or the first-place trophy, we all need to remember to emphasize the importance of the journey. You can model for parents how they can talk with their child about how it felt to work hard, encouraging them so that they use similar language when preparing for the next challenge.

Respect Each Child's Path

Our oldest boy started kindergarten like most children. He was excited about learning and couldn't wait to go to a real school. However, he struggled pretty much from the beginning. He couldn't spell, was a poor reader, and had difficulty focusing. Now I don't mean that he couldn't spell a word here and there. I mean that, no matter how many hours were spent preparing for his weekly spelling tests, he failed again and again. He learned, without question, that no amount of practice and studying was going to change the outcome. Fast forward through several schools, more failures, and many discipline issues, and he dropped out. Now before I continue this story, you should know that we tried to fill his cup with every positive thought we could. By this time, he had four parents who deeply loved him and wanted him to be successful. But it didn't matter. He learned from very early on that he couldn't do school and no amount of encouragement was going to change that.

Fast forward 2 more long and frustrating years . . . he's currently taking a full load of classes at a community college so that he can apply to the college of his dreams. He is more focused than we've ever seen him and is slowly building up his confidence. He has experienced first hand that he *can* meet the academic demands placed upon him and, although he still struggles like a typical student, his inner voice has taken on a much more positive tone. We like to video chat, and more often than not, we find him studying, and we could not be prouder of this young man. During our last conversation, he was telling us about his English assignment; he had to write an essay about what it means to be a gritty student (#notkidding).

Our boy took a hard path that no one would have chosen for him, but it was his path to take. Sure, hindsight is a luxury and we could have made fewer parenting mistakes, but we were steadfast in our support for and belief in him. It took him longer than we would have liked for him to develop the grit he needed to be successful, but so what? The point is that he is getting there.

As much as you are already exhausted from the meetings, planning, teaching, and the trillion other things you do every day, parents need to be reassured that every child's path is different and that it will be okay. You have the benefit of knowing their child in a different environment; use this opportunity to help them get to know other sides of their child. I can't tell you how many times I've had this awkward conversation:

Me: I just love Timmy! He is so witty and just has a great sense of humor.

Parent: Really? Timmy?

Me: (scanning my brain for Timmy's face to make sure I haven't confused him with someone else) Oh, yes. The other day he picked up on this very subtle, ironic situation that the other students missed. It was really fantastic and showed how much he pays attention to what's going on around him.

Parent: Wow. That is so interesting. He's always so serious at home.

Me: (smile and walk away)

Is it just me? Or have you also realized that you see a completely different side to your students than what their parents see? What a gift you can give to these parents to share that with them, particularly if you're highlighting the passion and perseverance that leads to grit. It also pays great dividends in building that relationship of trust and respect with your students (#winwin).

Set Routines

I'm guessing that you have routines in your classroom. Your students know how to turn their work in, where to find the supplies, how you start/end the day, etc. This is Teaching 101. Well, this is another teaching moment for you to help your parents. Remind them that it can be exhausting to be a kid, trying to figure out who you are and balancing responsibilities of school, home, and extracurricular activities. Establishing routines at home can provide a sense of balance that is often missed when rushing around from activity to activity. By setting dinner expectations, chore schedules, and bedtimes, parents are providing structures that don't require thought or reason. They also eliminate any potential struggle with children because they know what is expected. And, thank goodness, parents have less decisions to make on a daily basis because they have already established these routines.

> ## Remind parents that *gritty* children are often the product of parents who are consistent in their expectations.

Remind parents that *gritty* children are often the product of parents who are consistent in their expectations. They can only do that if they spend time with their children and with life's craziness, they have to fit that in where they can. Some days, maybe they eat dinner together. Other days, maybe "quality" time is during the carpool from school to home to practice. The non-negotiable is that they connect as a family; the how, when, and where are nonessential. Knowing this as a teacher can help facilitate conversations with parents about maintaining these connections in today's busy world.

Raise Kids so They Move Out

"I don't want to."
"Everyone else's parents let them quit."
"It's hard."
"It's no fun."

My kids have said all of these things numerous times. And guess what? I could say the same things about being a parent. But I made a commitment to this whole parenting gig and I'm sticking it out. (Truth be told, I'm waiting it out for that moment when they're in their 40s and they tell me I was right all along. I'll let you know how that works out. . . .) But the bottom line is this: Parents don't quit. You know why? Because I'm thinking about that time when one of my kids is 25 and just quits his job because he can't take another day. He has no back-up plan other than moving home so that he can "find himself." Uh, no. First of all, his room has been converted to the coziest of libraries (#15yearplan), and second of all, no.

If you think it's difficult to raise gritty kids, you're right. But what's the other option? You making oatmeal and doing the laundry of your grown daughter because she doesn't know how to work her way out of a struggle? No, thank you. So, this means parents have to do hard things. One of those things is that they have to let their child fight her own battles. Parents need to start this as early as possible. I love saving the day for my children, especially as they become more and more self-sufficient. It's nice to be needed, but mama has to have limits.

Parents need to teach their children how to handle conflict with a friend, approach a teacher about a low grade, work with people they don't like, and more:

- If a child forgets his homework at home, parents should not bring it to school.
- If he fails a test, parents should not e-mail the teacher asking how he can improve his grade.
- If he doesn't get much playing time on the basketball team, parents should not badmouth the coach.
- If he loses a library book, parents should not pay the fine without a plan for how he will work it off.

You get the point. Parents need to let their children develop the necessary skills for having difficult conversations, so that they grow into mature and responsible adults (who move out). Parents should want their children to save their own days, not look to their parents to always do the saving.

If you think it's difficult to raise gritty kids, you're right. But what's the other option?

Now, as a teacher, you know all of this. You roll your eyes when you get the e-mail from a helicopter mom or when Mary asks to call her mom to bring up her homework. But I can tell you that parents don't always know how to best handle these situations. First of all, their kid is calling and begging. Second of all, they don't like seeing their kids fail. And third, they think all of the other parents are doing all of these things for their kids and they don't want to be the "bad" parent. So give your parents this information. Tell them what is appropriate and what is not, given the age of your students. You are the expert—you deal with tons of kids of the same age every year. Help the parents out by getting them off the hook and setting the responsibility back onto the shoulders of their children. I promise they will love you for it. Let's start with Five Principles of Parenting a Gritty Kid. Repeat after me . . .

1. My child will have to face the consequences of forgetting something at home.
2. I will not intervene in an issue between my child and his teacher until my child has tried to handle it himself.
3. If my child commits to an activity (like joining a team or a club), he will finish the activity even if he wants to quit.
4. I will appropriately enforce the rules and expectations I set for my child.
5. If my child cries because she has a project due the next day and hasn't started it yet, I will support her, but I will not do it for her.

Note. First of all, there are always exceptions, so common sense is essential here. Second, there are about a thousand more principles I could add to this list, but hopefully these five give you the idea.

Final Thoughts

Raising kids is part joy and part guerilla warfare.
—Ed Asner

So this is where I give you a pep talk. I remind you that, while you didn't get your degree so that you could educate parents, that is exactly what you can and should be doing. I know you're tired, but this is crucial. Parents want what's best for their children. You want what's best for your students. To make this work, you have to establish a rock-solid partnership between school and home. Grit is a newish concept and while it's not difficult to understand, you will be at an advantage if you can build a positive, working relationship with parents before you start doing the hard things (i.e., holding kids accountable, pushing them toward excellence, etc.). You can do this! You can quietly get 20 first graders to use the restroom or give "the look" to an 6-foot-tall senior to get him to straighten up. You can do this, too.

Discussion Questions

1. How do you build positive relationships with the parents of your students?
2. Think of students who are being raised in each parenting style (authoritarian, permissive, and authoritative). How do you communicate/discipline/teach differently in response to this?
3. How can you share these ideas and suggestions for building grit with your parents? How can you support them along the way?

Chapter 7

Creating a Gritty School Culture

Because I love education so much, I thrive on professional development. I love leading and attending presentations. I also enjoy working with teachers to develop curriculum and explore innovative teaching strategies. But I absolutely do not enjoy traditional team-building activities. I don't want to create a skit about giving constructive feedback, and I don't want to dance to demonstrate the climate of my classroom. Sure, I'll talk about that stuff because I think it's valuable and efficient. But I'm out on the rest. All of that to say teachers have a variety of learning styles, just like students. And, although we are asking students to "fail forward," we also need to encourage faculty members to take risks, fail, and recover. The ideas of commitment, resilience, and putting passion into practice need to become a part of the *entire* school's culture.

Where do you go when you want to work out? When you want to be inspired? You don't go to the gym or a teacher's conference because it's convenient. You go because you want to surround yourself with likeminded people. Environment matters. It matters to you, an educator, just like it matters to your students. If you want your students to be gritty, you need to establish a school culture that breeds passion and perseverance.

DOI: 10.4324/9781003235385-7

Even more, where do you go when you realize that you've fallen short of your goals? Well, if you want to feel better about yourself, you probably reach out to someone who will comfort you and remind you that you're fabulous just the way you are. If you want to get through this setback and keep pushing forward, you go to someone with similar goals as you. When I start feeling icky about my health, I turn to my friends who will hold me accountable to eating healthy and working out—not my mom who will just tell me I'm beautiful and give me cake (#loveher).

It's the same in school. It needs to be a place where making mistakes and failing is just something we do because that's a stepping stone on the path to success. Mary Cay Ricci (2015) suggested that we encourage students to talk about their "epic fails" and (I love this one) we view failures as data. All we're doing is gathering information about what doesn't work so that we can figure out what does. There is no judgment—just data.

According to Habegger (2008), "School culture is the heart of improvement and growth" (p. 42). It's the compilation of school norms, shared beliefs, meaningful ceremonies, traditions, and stories (Education World, 1996–2017). Just like the feeling you get when you spend time in someone's home and can describe it as cozy or frigid, you can feel the culture by walking the halls and visiting with staff and students. It is created by establishing a vision for the school that is supported by teachers and students.

When my stepson reported to his college baseball coaches for the first time, he was given very clear expectations. The players were to only wear clothing that positively portrayed their commitment to their team. They were no longer from a variety of high schools or club teams; they were *one* team. This belief in the team was one part of creating a championship culture.

Duckworth (2016) interviewed Lieutenant General Robert Caslen, West Point's superintendent. General Caslen described what he called a developmental model of retaining West Point cadets during the grueling Beast Barracks, West Point's version of basic training. In the developmental model, General Caslen explained the importance of leading from the front. Leading from the front refers to being in the middle of the action, holding everyone accountable to the same high standards. These leaders treat everyone at every level with respect and provide them all with the support they need to be successful. Let's look a little further to see how we can transfer this idea of "leading from the front" to our schools.

Supportive and Demanding Leadership

At the heart of a gritty school culture is a demanding and supportive leadership team. The administrators set high expectations for their teachers and vice versa. The teachers set high expectations for their students and vice versa. The school is a synergy of people of all ages, all in pursuit of excellence.

With a leadership department committed to cultivating grit, teachers must be accountable to this. To begin, accountability is not scary and it's *very* important that this be communicated to all faculty. Accountability is not a way to "catch" teachers and students or to be punitive in any way; it's merely placing a priority on grit. And how do we show our priorities? By spending time on them, of course.

Teachers spend a great deal of time developing curriculum and writing lesson plans, but consider how much time is spent evaluating these plans. Well, if the expectation is that grit development is infused in lessons, then this should be a topic of discussion, a "grit check." It goes something like this: Every Tuesday, a campus leader meets with the math teachers. Essential information is communicated, student concerns are discussed, and weekly lessons are grit checked. In a grit check, the teacher describes how he or she is providing opportunities for students to cultivate passion and/or persevere through challenges. Fellow teachers respond with constructive feedback and encouragement. If a meeting is not feasible (because, let's face it, sometimes we can't handle *one. more. meeting.*), this can be done electronically. Create a simple template, pair up teachers, and the grit check can happen within 5 minutes or so online. It's quick, easy, and a tenable reminder of this commitment to establishing a gritty school culture. Figure 9 includes examples of questions to ask during a grit check.

> # It's not enough to stand in front your staff and pronounce, "Go and be gritty."

Remember the "vice versa" part of accountability that I mentioned earlier? Well, administrators need to be accountable as well. It's not enough to stand in front your staff and pronounce, "Go and be gritty." As a director, principal, or other kind of leader, consider what you can do to cultivate passion and perseverance in your staff. You should absolutely recognize and celebrate individual passions; however, we are in the school business and you can likely assume that the people who work with you are passionate about kids and education. (I mean . . . why else would they show up every day? Seriously.) As a leader, it is your responsibility to extricate that passion and to kindle it in every person on your campus.

Provide Opportunities

Provide opportunities for your staff members to be leaders and to share their passion with others. Be sure to consider all of your teachers, not just the ones who gravitate toward leadership roles. You've got to hook the ones in the back, too. If you know you have teachers who are crazy for data, ask them to be a part of your data mining and disaggregation activities. The same with lesson design, recycling, social-emotional needs of students, dealing with parents, etc. However, understand that a teacher's most precious commodity is time and she is not going to give that up if the trade is not important.

- Where are you emphasizing passion in your students?
- What is the "so what" of your lesson?
- At what point do you think your students will struggle?
- What is your plan of action for when/if your students want to give up?
- Is there something about this lesson that needs to be communicated to parents in order to support the objective?
- Can you think of any students for which this lesson will be too easy? How will you handle that?
- What happens if your students just don't care about the content of this lesson?
- How can you connect this lesson to what your students do care about?

FIGURE 9. *Sample grit check questions.*

Meetings

We have to talk about meetings. Don't set up a meeting unless it is imperative and the most efficient way to share the information. If the meeting can be an e-mail, send an e-mail. If there is an issue that only pertains to part of the staff, only meet with that part of the staff. And schedule your meetings appropriately. I've already told you that I don't like the faux-engaging activities where I have to make a poster or write a poem about the climate of my classroom. If you ask me to do that on a Wednesday after school, I'm going through the motions just to get out of there. If you ask me to do that during the week that grades are due, I'm trying to saw my finger off with the tip of my pen just to get out of there (and run to the hospital).

> Don't set up a meeting unless it is imperative and the most efficient way to share the information

Additionally, be sure that the agenda and purpose are clear to the participants. This really is important. There is nothing worse than going into a meeting that you thought was a quick update on a field trip and it's actually a grit check or a meeting with a parent (#blindsided). Meeting norms should be established that outline expectations for unconditional respect, appropriate use of technology, start and end times, etc. The culture of your meetings needs to reflect the culture of your school.

The other half of grit is perseverance. This is a little more difficult than everyone getting on board with passion. I mean, passion is fun and exciting. Perseverance is . . . hard. First of all, in order to persevere you have to be presented with a challenge. We already know that school staff have the passion for kids and education needed to overcome challenges, so now it comes down to the obstacles.

Obstacles

Hmm. There are plenty: lack of supplies, emphasis on testing, lack of support, etc. I hear you. I feel you. There is no shortage of obstacles, but the reason why teachers burn out and don't persevere through these is that we can't ever "overcome" those. As educational leaders, administrators need to emphasize what staff members can control and present those as the most important obstacles. Sure, there are things we have to do as part of the job, but the priority should be placed on taking educational risks, teaching content in a new way, and building authentic relationships with students.

Every child, even (and especially) the difficult ones, deserves a person at school who can advocate for him.

We also know that students face a variety of obstacles; some are obvious and some aren't. Either way, treat every student as if he is dealing with some kind of crisis and treat him with the same kindness and unconditional respect that you treat one another. Every child, even (and especially) the difficult ones, deserves a person at school who can advocate for him.

Communication and Discipline

Communication of the kind of culture, and what grit means, is essential to building and maintaining a gritty school culture. Create an expression or a call back that everyone can memorize. For example, pick a sport, and watch an elite team warm up. Watch them huddle before the start of the game. Hear one player call out and other players respond in unison. It's likely that the response reflects a core value of that team. Maybe they yell, "Teamwork," "Win," or "Defense." The same is true of the military and churches. They respond with different things, but this ritual is important to the culture.

Ensure that everyone at every level understands that your school is a place where people "go for it," where no one holds back and no one gives up. If a first grader says she wants to be an artist when she grows up, why would you *not* tell her to go for it? Is there a point in committing to something and practicing it with a heart full of hope and experiencing the pure joy of doing it? Yes. That's why I run. I'll never run in the Olympics, but I still lace up my tennis shoes every chance I get. Running relaxes me and keeps me healthy, benefits that are completely worth my time and effort. Similarly, although a goal in talent development is to build elite performers, it's crucial to also focus on what you gain along the way.

> Ensure that everyone at every level understands that your school is a place where people go for it, where no one holds back and no one gives up.

In her 2015 book, *Ready-to-Use Resources for Mindsets in the Classroom: Everything Educators Need for Building Growth Mindset Learning Communities*, Ricci developed myriad resources for cultivating a "growth mindset school culture." This includes the development of psychosocial skills—perseverance, grit, resiliency, and the ability to learn from failure—in students. Figure 10 is an example of a chart in which to record a school- or districtwide plan to develop these noncognitive factors in students. This is something you and your staff could work together to develop.

Both Ricci (2015) and Dweck (2014) emphasized the power of "yet." By focusing on the yet, we are making room to celebrate progress, not just success. That is essential to creating a culture of grit. School has to be a place where we all push ourselves and work harder than the day before, while also being the place where we celebrate our growth over time.

Along this line, positive and restorative discipline can be used to refocus staff and students on the culture and goals of the school. Restorative discipline is the practice of holding students accountable to exhibiting self-control and being engaged and inclusive. Rather than punitive, students are involved in the disciplinary process by reflecting, practicing empathy, and setting goals for improvement. The language associated with grit (i.e., passion, interests, overcoming obstacles, perseverance, etc.) should be included in the discipline language with students; this language should also be a part of conversations with teachers about improving their practice.

RESOURCE 1

Deliberate Cultivation of Noncognitive Factors

School/Office/Program: _____ Date: _____

Psychosocial Skill	Actions Our School/District Has Already Taken to Cultivate These Skills	Ideas to Cultivate Noncognitive Factors	Ideas for Monitoring and Measuring Progress in This Area
Perseverance			
Grit			
Resiliency			
Learning From Failure			

FIGURE 10. *Deliberate cultivation of noncognitive factors. From* Ready-to-Use Resources for Mindsets in the Classroom: Everything Educators Need for Building Growth Mindset Learning Communities *(p. 5), by M. C. Ricci, 2015, Waco, TX: Taylor & Francis Group Copyright 2015 by Taylor & Francis Group Reprinted with permission.*

Creating a Gritty School Culture

Daily Rituals and Routines

Rituals and routines are another crucial component of establishing a strong school culture. Many schools already have routines in place (i.e., where students go before school, how students behave in the hall, etc.). Routines provide comfort and stability, two characteristics that are imperative for growth and development (regardless of age). Routines can also be used to address discipline issues; examine your classroom or school for gaps and then put habits in place to bridge those gaps.

I was fortunate to work for three outstanding principals and learned so much from each of them. For most of my career I worked with one man. One of his favorite sentiments was, "What gets recognized gets repeated." He absolutely believed this and he walked the walk. His message during staff meetings was to build relationships with our students and to focus on the individual greatness in each of them. He encouraged teachers to recognize students for their positive choices. Anytime teachers volunteered to help with a dance or sponsor a club, he made sure to recognize us with a certificate or an announcement. People like being told that they are doing a good job, and most of us are simple enough that we will keep doing that behavior so that we get praised again. What gets recognized gets repeated.

Effort and Passion

You've heard that passion comes from within. And that passion is the thing that keeps you up at night. But what if you don't have anything related to passion "within" you and you sleep fine at night? Luckily, that doesn't mean that you are destined for a passionless life. It does mean that you may need exposure to new ideas and activities. We can cover some, but not all, of this in the core curriculum.

If you want to build a culture of grit, you cannot do it without offering electives and structured free time to your students. Offer electives—as many as possible. The electives should be as rigorous as core classes. No blow-off classes. Know the difference between, "This class is easy," and "I'm so interested in this class that I don't even mind working hard."

> # If you want to build a culture of grit, you cannot do it without offering electives and structured free time to your students.

I'm going to write a sentence now that may hurt your heart a bit. It hurt mine. "School settings appeared to undermine rather than support passion" (Fredricks, Alfeld, & Eccles, 2010, p. 26). Doesn't that make you want to cry? Now, this statement was a result of one study, but still. . . . The authors of the study compared gifted and nongifted students and found that gifted students were bored and not-at-all passionate in their classes because they felt the material was taught at lower levels. This did not occur when gifted students were taught with students of similar ability, which supports prior research in this area (Hertzog, 2003). In fact, grouping similar students together is the easiest and most effective way to challenge and support gifted learners (Rogers, 2006).

Fredricks, Alfeld, and Eccles (2010) provided six suggestions for how school staff members can cultivate passion and create a culture of grit. Lucky for you, because you've gotten this far into the book, these support the case I have been making for building grit in the classroom. Here they are:

1. **Be enthusiastic.** Love your content, your students, and your school—and show it.
2. **Care.** Whether they are 5 or 15, your students want to know that you care about them. You are interested in their lives outside of school and, as cheesy as it sounds, are chal-

lenging them because you care so much. As a teacher, you also need to make it clear that your classroom is a community of learners that cares about, supports, and respectfully challenges one another. It is not a place where we degrade or bully others.

3. **Align content delivery to students' needs.** Some students need a lecture with closed notes. Others need an open-ended objective, a computer, and a quiet space. You should be using different methods to teach your material because your students are . . . well, different.

4. **Require students to engage with the content.** Start at the bottom of Bloom's (1956) taxonomy and work your way up. This part is messy and difficult (hint: optimal grit-building opportunity).

5. **Regularly offer specific feedback.** Throughout this book I've made constant comparisons between academic and athletic and military settings. Feedback is another disparate area within these domains. In school, particularly core classes, feedback is often provided after the assignment is completed. I know there is a difference between watching a team execute a football play and teaching students to write an essay. However, although you are pushing and challenging your students so they have opportunities to persevere, you have to be there to scaffold and encourage along the way. Otherwise you might lose them altogether.

6. **Challenge students.** Ah. We understand "challenge" and we know what that looks like. But challenging students can be difficult, especially when there are a variety of abilities in one classroom. It also makes life harder for the teacher because you have to stay that much more ahead of your students. But, you're a teacher and you can do anything.

Now take a look back at those six suggestions, but this time read them from the perspective of an administrator. Replace "students" with "staff" and you have specific guidelines for building a culture of grit. I know, you're probably wondering why it took me so long to get to these, but I had to get you to buy into this before I could lay them all out for you. Plus, wasn't this fun?

Final Thoughts

Culture is simply a shared way of doing something with a passion.

—Brian Chesky

You can think about establishing a culture of grit in three ways. You start at the bottom, building grit with your students and hope it moves up the ranks. You start at the top, with administrators celebrating the gritty behaviors they see in their staff and hope it trickles down to the students. Or, you can bookend the process by focusing on creating gritty students and gritty teachers. You know what happens, right? The gritty attitudes and behaviors are going to skyrocket up and shoot down, squeezing out the ones in the middle who aren't ready for this. And that's okay, because you have a job to do and you need everyone on board in order to be successful.

Discussion Questions

1. How would you describe the current culture of your school?
2. What are some practical ways for promoting passion and perseverance among students and staff?
3. How will you measure a change in your school's culture?

Conclusion

We've known forever that hard work is a key component to success, and, over time, schools have pivoted between focusing on cultivating passion and increasing rigor. Grit has captivated the attention of teachers—especially those of us who are . . . ahem . . . seasoned—for quite some time because it encompasses our need to keep the joy in learning while maintaining high standards. But I would be living on a unicorn farm (how great would that be?) if I believed that everyone was on the grit train with me. So, I'm going to load up the unicorns, and we can talk about potential issues related to the concept of grit. I pulled quotes from three different articles that capture some of the existing critiques of the construct. Take a look . . .

> If we want to improve a child's grit or resilience or self-control, it turns out that the place to begin is not with the child himself. What we need to change first, it seems, is his environment. (Tough, 2016, p. 12)

In his article, Paul Tough (2016) introduced two important ideas. First, he highlighted the problem with teaching a psychosocial skill (like grit) in the same way that we teach academic content (like math). He is absolutely correct in that you cannot sit down

139

with students, define the terms of grit, and then expect them to just go and be gritty. He described teachers he encountered in his research who helped develop admirable character quality without even using the words "respect," "integrity," etc. It was the calculated implementation of quality learning experiences that led to the development of these character traits.

That first point leads into Tough's (2016) second point: the importance of environment on developing soft skills like grit. Tough uses "environment" in his article, although I argue for "culture." These may seem like they're the same. I would argue, however, that culture more accurately reflects a model that is conducive to cultivating grit because *culture* is more than a physical place. It includes administration, custodial staff, parents, teachers, and students. Furthermore, when conceptualizing a culture, we think of constructing it from the inside out; it's an active process involving all stakeholders and not just something that is done from the outside. And, in that case, we do begin with the child him- or herself.

> *[G]rit research may have fallen victim to the jangle fallacy and that grit as currently measured is simply a repackaging of conscientiousness or one of the facets of conscientiousness. (Credé, Tynan, & Harms, 2016, p. 11)*

Conscientiousness is one of the "Big Five" personality traits and is often cited as the trait most predictive of academic and job-related success (Judge, Higgins, Thoresen, & Barrick, 1999). A person with high conscientiousness is one who is responsible, organized, and exhibits self-control (Costa, McCrae, & Dye, 1991). Sounds like grit, right? Right. But, as you probably realize, conscientiousness does not encapsulate all that it means to be gritty. What about the passion? The emotional intensity that allows someone to persevere through intense challenges? Although Crede and his research team (2016) indicated that grit *may* be related to a component of conscientiousness, it is important to not lose sight of the distinctive nature of grit. It is not a simple "repackaging," nor is it the panacea of achievement. Grit is a construct, built upon prior psychological research, with a place in our schools.

> *The physiological and psychological toll of grit is particularly pronounced in adults from disadvantaged backgrounds, who are minorities, who lack the financial and social capital to get through the trials of everyday life. (Kashdan, 2017, sec. 2, para. 2)*

Kashdan's (2017) article is fascinating, particularly his comparison between grit and John Henryism. (John Hennryism is the result of a famous legend. The folk tale tells the story of a slave, John Henry, who is convinced that he can work harder and faster than a steam drill. In the end [spoiler alert!] he beats the steam drill, but dies from exhaustion.) Kashdan's point is an important one: We will be in serious trouble if we forget the humanity of teaching and only emphasize rigor and extreme effort. Our students, particularly those who may be disadvantaged, become casualties if we are negligent in supporting their psychological needs. When pursuing excellence, it's natural to feel self-doubt, stress, exhaustion, anxiety, and a whole host of other complicated emotions. So if you're committed to building a culture of grit, you need to be equally committed to providing the social-emotional support your students need, especially those who are disadvantaged. That's what it means to be all in, folks.

Grit is not *the* solution to the issues you may be experiencing in the classroom; it is one way to conceive of the effort and skill needed to achieve at high levels. Understanding grit provides the context we need to understand why both rigor and passion are so important to include in our curriculum. Knowing what you now know about the implications of persistent effort, you can begin to think about how you can provide regular opportunities for your students to struggle their way through problems.

You know the importance of a gritty school culture, of building the capacity for a school full of people (and their parents) to support each other as they strive for excellence. You understand how grit aligns with our prior understanding of mindsets and learning orientations. You have practical ideas for nurturing curiosity as if it were a standard of our curriculum. Most of all, I hope you are invigorated and inspired to go to the next level, to set and pursue your stretch goals, and to be the absolute best for every student every day. You've got this.

Resources

Creativity and Passion

Bean. (n.d.). *Interest surveys*. Retrieved from http://usugtsharefair. weebly.com/uploads/2/6/0/9/26092725/bean_environment. pdf

Check this out for 15 different interest inventories!

Briggs, S. (2013). *25 ways to institute passion-based learning in the classroom* [Web log post]. Retrieved from http://www.open colleges.edu.au/informed/features/25-ways-to-institute-passion-based-learning-in-the-classroom

Take a look at this practical list. It's a great reminder that it's really not too hard to cultivate passion in school!

GenerationOn. (2011). *Youth interest inventory*. Retrieved from http://www.generationon.org/files/flat-page/files/youth_ interest_inventory_1.pdf

This link provides three interest inventories—one for elementary, one for middle, and one for high school. The questions are open-ended, so the possibilities are endless for students' responses. I recommend having students complete the inventory and then wait a few weeks and have them revisit it to see if they can add to their responses.

Maiers, A., & Sandvold, A. (2011). *The passion-driven classroom: A framework for teaching and learning.* London, England: Routledge.

Angela Maiers and Amy Sandvold are so incredibly passionate about passion! This comes through in this practical text—you'll love it.

McNair, A. (2017). *Genius hour: Passion projects that ignite innovation and student inquiry.* Waco, TX: Prufrock Press.

This resource is perfect if you want to jump right into Genius Hour.

Piirto, J. (Ed.). (2014). *Organic creativity in the classroom: Teaching to intuition in academics and the arts.* Waco, TX: Prufrock Press.

Jane Piirto is a legend in the field of creativity. This edited book provides glimpses into creativity in the classroom from multiple perspectives. I cowrote a chapter about creativity in language arts that is pretty fantastic.

Renzulli, J. S., & Reis, S. M. (n.d.). *SEM third edition resources and forms.* Retrieved from http://gifted.uconn.edu/schoolwide-enrichment-model/sem3rd

Holy cow! Every resource you could ever want about the Schoolwide Enrichment Model is provided on this website. It's free and high quality.

Design Thinking

Spencer, J., & Juliani, A. J. (2016). *Launch: Using design thinking to boost creativity and bring out the maker in every student.* San Diego, CA: Burgess Consulting.

Design thinking is a newer concept—the authors of this book really break it down for us to implement with our students.

Wise, S. (2016). *Design thinking in education: Empathy, challenge, discovery, and sharing* [Web log post]. Retrieved from https://www.edutopia.org/blog/design-thinking-empathy-challenge-discovery-sharing-susie-wise

This is an excellent introduction to the beauty and possibility of design thinking. Start here!

Differentiation

Byrd, I. (n.d.). The differentiator. *Byrdseed.* Retrieved from http://byrdseed.com/differentiator

First of all, I love the name of this, "The Differentiator." Second of all, it's this magic way for you to get ideas (good ideas) for how to differentiate for your students. It's addicting to play around with this tool.

Cash, R. M. (2017). *Advancing differentiation: Thinking and learning for the 21st century* (Rev. ed.). Minneapolis, MN: Free Spirit.

This text provides modern, practical, and rigorous (and research-based) ideas for differentiating your content. It's a gem.

iNACOL Staff. (2016). *What is blended learning?* [Web log post]. Retrieved from http://www.inacol.org/news/what-is-blended-learning

Personalized learning isn't as hard as it sounds. This is a great introduction to what it is and how you can do this, along with everything else you're required to do.

Miller, A. (2012). *Blended learning: strategies for engagement* [Web log post]. Retrieved from https://www.edutopia.org/blog/blended-learning-engagement-strategies-andrew-miller

Miller's blog post provides practical ways for you to authentically leverage technology to engage your students. It's great!

Sanguras, L. Y. (2016). Blended learning: A new frontier of differentiated curriculum. In T. Kettler (Ed.), *Modern curriculum for gifted and advanced academic students* (pp. 237–250). Waco, TX: Prufrock Press.

I'm a big proponent of blended and personalized learning. I wrote about that here.

Grit

Duckworth, A. (2016). *Grit: The power of passion and perseverance.* New York, NY: Scribner.

Duckworth's book is the basis for what I know about grit. It's an easy and engaging read. It just might set your teacher soul on fire!

Tough, P. (2013). *How children succeed: Grit, curiosity, and the hidden power of character.* New York, NY: Mariner Books.

Tough's book is another goodie. He draws parallels between grit and social-emotional learning.

Growth Mindset

Dweck, C. S. (2007). *Mindset: The new psychology of success.* New York, NY: Ballantine Books.

Dweck is the one to know when studying mindsets. Her work is highly regarded and is the place to start if you want to study this concept further.

Ricci, M. C. (2015). *Ready-to-use resources for mindsets in the classroom: Everything educators need for school success.* Waco, TX: Prufrock Press.

This resource book is really great. Ricci takes Dweck's work and highlights practical ways we can implement what we know about mindsets in the classroom.

Talent Development

Duke TIP—https://tip.duke.edu

The Duke Talent Identification Program (TIP) is known for its talent searches. Its website also provides resources for working with gifted students.

Johns Hopkins Center for Talented Youth—http://cty.jhu.edu

The Center for Talented Youth (CTY) is another talent search organization. It offers summer and online programs; plus, the website offers websites for parents and teachers of gifted students.

Northwestern Center for Talent Development—https://www.ctd.northwestern.edu

The Center for Talent Development offers programs to gifted students. I like its newsletter because it connects research to practice in a way that's helpful to teachers.

Subotnik, R. F., Olszewski-Kubilius, P., & Worrell, F. C. (2011). Rethinking giftedness and gifted education: A proposed direction forward based on psychological science.

Psychological Science in the Public Interest, 12, 3–54. doi:10.
1177.1529100611418029.

Here is the infamous paper that articulates giftedness in a way that
blew me away several years ago. This is the final resource in this
list, but it was really where my thoughts on grit began.

References

Alexander, R. (1988). A town celebrates the lowly lima bean. *The New York Times*. Retrieved from http://www.nytimes.com/1988/10/19/garden/a-town-celebrates-the-lowly-lima-bean.html

Barker, E. (2016). *This is how to resist distraction: 4 secrets to remarkable focus* [Web log post]. Retrieved from http://www.bakadesuyo.com/2016/10/how-to-resist-distraction

Baum, J. R., & Locke, E. A. (2004). The relationship of entrepreneurial traits, skill, and motivation to subsequent venture growth. *Journal of Applied Psychology, 89,* 587–598. doi:10.1037/0021-9010.89.4.587

Baumrind, D. (1966). Effects of authoritative parental control on child behavior. *Child Development, 37,* 887–907.

Bird, B. J. (1989). *Entrepreneurial behavior.* Glenview, IL: Scott, Foresman.

Bloom, B. S. (Ed.). (1956). *Taxonomy of educational objectives: The classification of educational goals. Handbook I: Cognitive domain.* New York, NY: Longmans Green.

Bloom, B. S. (1985). *Developing talent in young people.* New York, NY: Ballantine Books.

Boyd, B. (2016). Leonard Cohen: The key songs and what they mean. *The Irish Times.* Retrieved from http://www.irishtimes.

com/culture/music/leonard-cohen-the-key-songs-and-what-they-mean-1.2864114

California Department of Education. (2015). *NGSS for California Public Schools, K–12*. Retrieved from http://www.cde.ca.gov/pd/ca/sc/ngssstandards.asp

Caprara, G. V., Vecchione, M., Alessandri, G., Gerbino, M., & Barbaranelli, C. (2011). The contribution of personality traits and self-efficacy beliefs to academic achievement: A longitudinal study. *British Journal of Educational Psychology, 81,* 78–96.

Carroll, J. B. (1997). Psychometrics, intelligence, and public perception. *Intelligence, 24,* 25–52. http://dx.doi.org/10.1016/S0160-2896(97)90012-X

Clark, W. H. (1935). Two tests for perseverance. *Journal of Educational Psychology, 26,* 604–610. http://dx.doi.org/10.1037/h0053523

Coleman, L. J., & Guo, A. (2013). Exploring children's passion for learning in six domains. *Journal for the Education of the Gifted, 36,* 155–175. doi:10.1177/0162353213480432

Collins, B. (1996). *Introduction to poetry*. Retrieved from https://www.poetryfoundation.org/poems-and-poets/poems/detail/46712

Costa, P. T., Jr., McCrae, R. R., & Dye, D. A. (1991). Facet scales for agreeableness and conscientiousness: A revision of the NEO Personality Inventory. *Personality and Individual Differences, 12,* 887–898.

Credé, M., Tynan, M. C., & Harms, P. D. (2016). Much ado about grit: A meta-analytic synthesis of the grit literature. *Journal of Personality and Social Psychology.* doi: 10.1037/pspp0000102

Daniels, H. (Ed.). (2005). *An introduction to Vygotsky*. New York, NY: Psychology Press.

Dewar, G. (2011–2015). Teaching self-control: Evidence-based tips. *Parenting Science.* Retrieved from http://www.parentingscience.com/teaching-self-control.html

Duckworth, A. (2016). *Grit: The power of passion and perseverance*. New York, NY: Scribner.

Duckworth, A. L. (2013). *Angela Lee Duckworth: Grit: The power of passion and perseverance* [Video file]. Retrieved from https://www.ted.com/talks/angela_lee_duckworth_grit_the_power_of_passion_and_perseverance

Duckworth, A. L., & Gross, J. J. (2014). Self-control and grit: Related but separable determinants of success. *Current Directions in Psychological Science, 23,* 319–325.

Duckworth, A. L., Peterson, C., Matthews, M. D., & Kelly, D. R. (2007). Grit: Perseverance and passion for long-term goals. *American Psychological Association, 92,* 1087–1101. doi:10.10 37/0022-3514.92.6.1087

Duckworth, A. L., & Seligman, M. E. P. (2005). Self-discipline outdoes IQ in predicting academic performance of adolescents. *Psychological Science, 16,* 939–944.

Dweck, C. S. (2006). *Mindset: The new psychology of success.* New York, NY: Random House.

Dweck, C. S. (2014). *The power of yet: Carol S. Dweck: TEDxNor rköping* [Video file]. Retrieved from https://www.youtube.com/watch?v=J-swZaKN2Ic

Education World. (1996–2017). Is your school's culture toxic or positive? *Education World.* Retrieved from http://www.educationworld.com/a_admin/admin/admin275.shtml

Fredricks, A. F., Alfeld, C., & Eccles, J. (2010). Developing and fostering passion in academic and nonacademic domains. *Gifted Child Quarterly, 54,* 18–30. doi:10.1177/0016986209352683

Freud, S. (1920). *Introductory lectures on psychoanalysis.* New York, NY: Norton.

frog. (2012). The paradox of passion. *designmind.* Retrieved from http://designmind.frogdesign.com/2012/08/paradox-passion

Galton, F. (1869/2006). *Hereditary genius: An inquiry into its laws and consequences.* London, England: Macmillan.

Gardner, H. E. (2000). *Intelligence reframed: Multiple intelligences for the 21st century.* New York, NY: Basic Books.

Gottfredson, L. S. (1998). The general intelligence factor. *Scientific American Presents, 9*(4), 24–29.

Grantham, T. C., & Ford, D. Y. (2003). Beyond self-concept and self-esteem: Racial identity and gifted African American students. *The High School Journal, 87,* 18–29.

Habegger, S. (2008). The principal's role in successful schools: Creating a positive school culture. *Principal, 88(1),* 42–46.

Hertzog, N. B. (2003). Impact of gifted programs from the students' perspectives. *Gifted Child Quarterly, 47,* 131–143.

Hofmann, W., Luhmann, M., Fisher, R. R., Vohs, K. D., & Baumeister, R. F. (2013). Yes, but are they happy? Effects of trait self-control on affective well-being and life satisfaction. *Journal of Personality, 82,* 265–277. doi:10.1111/jopy.12050

Hyslop, G. (2016). The most basic thing millennials can do to impress their bosses. *Fortune.* Retrieved from http://fortune.com/2016/09/15/millennials-perseverance-boeing

IDEO. (2017). *Design thinking.* Retrieved from https://www.ideou.com/pages/design-thinking

James, W. (1890). *The principles of psychology* (Vol. 1). New York, NY: Holt and Company.

Jensen, A. R. (1980). Chronometric analysis of intelligence. *Journal of Social and Biological Structures, 3,* 103–122. http://dx.doi.org/10.1016/0140-1750(80)90003-2

Judge, T. A., Higgins, C. A., Thoresen, C. J., & Barrick, M. R. (1999). The big five personality traits, general mental ability, and career success across the life span. *Personnel Psychology, 52,* 621–652.

Kantrowitz, A. (2013). Five highlights from Commander Chris Hadfield's Reddit AMA from space. *Forbes.* Retrieved from http://www.forbes.com/sites/alexkantrowitz/2013/02/18/five-highlights-from-commander-chris-hadfields-reddit-ama-from-space/#2eeba24320f6

Kashdan, T. B. (2017). *How I learned about the perils of grit: Rethinking simple explanations for complicated problems* [Web log post]. Retrieved from https://www.psychologytoday.com/blog/curious/201704/how-i-learned-about-the-perils-grit

Kerr, B. A., & Multon, K. D. (2015). The development of gender identity, gender roles, and gender relations in gifted students. *Journal of Counseling & Development, 93,* 183–191.

Kesler, E. (n.d.). *Genius hour.* Retrieved from http://www.genius hour.com

Kettler, T. (Ed.). (2016). *Modern curriculum for gifted and advanced academic students.* Waco, TX: Prufrock Press.

Kohn, A. (1999). *Punished by rewards: The trouble with gold stars, incentive plans, A's, praise, and other bribes* (2nd ed.). New York, NY: Mariner Books.

Krakovsky, M. (2007). The effort effect. *Stanford Magazine, 36*(2), 46–52.

Lebowitz, S. (2016a). A UPenn psychologist says there's one trait more important to success or IQ or talent. *Business Insider.* Retrieved from http://www.businessinsider.com/angela-duckworth-grit-more-important-than-iq-or-talent-2016-5

Lebowitz, S. (2016b). A top psychologist says there's only one way to become the best in your field—but not everyone agrees. *Business Insider.* Retrieved from http://www.business insider.com/anders-ericsson-how-to-become-an-expert-at-anything-2016-6

Lebowitz, S. (2016c). If you're having fun practicing, you're doing it wrong—no matter what you're trying to learn. *Business Insider.* Retrieved from http://nordic.businessinsider.com/anders-ericsson-becoming-an-expert-is-not-enjoyable-2016-6

Lowin, R. (2016). This goat with anxiety only calms down when she's in a duck costume. *Today.* Retrieved from http://www.today.com/pets/goat-anxiety-only-calms-down-when-duck-costume-t105482

Lowry, L. (2011). *Number the stars.* Boston, MA: HMH Books for Young Readers.

Luna, E., & The Great Discontent. (2017). #The100DayProject. *The Great Discontent.* Retrieved from https://thegreatdiscontent.com/100days

Maier, S. F., & Seligman, M. E. (1976). Learned helplessness: Theory and evidence. *Journal of Experimental Psychology: General, 105*, 3–46.

McCabe, M. (2016). MSU football recruit recalls journey from war-torn Iraq. *Detroit Free Press*. Retrieved from http://usatodayhss.com/2016/dearborns-mustafa-khaleefah-a-quick-study-in-football

McNair, A. (2017). *Genius hour: Passion projects that ignite innovation and student inquiry.* Waco, TX: Prufrock Press.

Mehta, J. (2015). *Breadth and depth: Can we have it both ways?* [Web log post]. Retrieved from http://blogs.edweek.org/edweek/learning_deeply/2015/07/breadth_and_depth_can_we_have_it_both_ways.html.

Minutaglio, R. (2016, September 15). Georgia college student and 4-time cancer survivor pursues passion to teach: 'This disease doesn't define me.' *People*. Retrieved from http://people.com/celebrity/kennedy-cobble-overcame-cancer-4-times-to-pursue-teaching-passion

National Association for Gifted Children. (n.d.). *Identification.* Retrieved from https://www.nagc.org/resources-publications/gifted-education-practices/identification

National Association for Gifted Children. (2010). *Redefining giftedness for a new century: Shifting the paradigm* [Position Statement]. Retrieved from http://www.nagc.org/sites/default/files/Position%20Statement/Redefining%20Giftedness%20for%20a%20New%20Century.pdf

Newport, C. (2012). Why 'follow your passion' is bad advice. *CNN*. Retrieved from http://edition.cnn.com/2012/08/29/opinion/passion-career-cal-newport

Ohio Department of Education. (2017). *Ohio's learning standards for mathematics.* Retrieved from https://education.ohio.gov/getattachment/Topics/Learning-in-Ohio/Mathematics/Ohio-s-Learning-Standards-in-Mathematics/MATH-Standards-2017.pdf.aspx

Olszewski Kubilius, P., Subotnik, R. F., & Worrell, F. C. (2015). Conceptualizations about giftedness and the development of talent: Implications for counselors. *Journal of Counseling and Development, 93,* 143–152.

Petty, T., & Lynn, J. (1989). I won't back down [Recorded by Tom Petty and the Heartbreakers]. On *Full Moon Fever* [CD]. MCA Records.

Pink, D. H. (2011). *Drive: The surprising truth about what motivates us.* New York, NY: Riverhead Books.

Ramirez, A. (2013). Passion-based learning [Web log post]. Retrieved from https://www.edutopia.org/blog/passion-based-learning-ainissa-ramirez

Renzulli, J. S. (1984, April). *The three ring conception of giftedness: A developmental model for creative productivity.* Paper presented at the annual meeting of the American Educational Research Association, New Orleans.

Renzulli, J. S., & Reis, S. M. (2014). *The schoolwide enrichment model: A how-to guide for talent development* (3rd ed.). Waco, TX: Prufrock Press.

Ricci, M. C. (2013). *Mindsets in the classroom: Building a culture of success and student achievement in school.* Waco, TX: Prufrock Press.

Ricci, M. C. (2015). *Ready-to-use resources for mindsets in the classroom: Everything educators need for school success.* Waco, TX: Prufrock Press.

Roid, G. H. (2003). *Stanford-Binet Intelligence Scales* (5th ed.). Itasca, IL: Riverside.

Rogers, K. B. (2006). *A menu of options for grouping gifted students.* Waco, TX: Prufrock Press.

Smith, A. K., Mick, E., & Faraone, S. V. (2009). Advances in genetic studies of Attention-Deficit/Hyperactivity Disorder. *Current Psychiatry Reports, 11,* 143–148.

Spearman, C. (1904). "General intelligence," objectively determined and measured. *The American Journal of Psychology, 15,* 201–292.

Subotnik, R. F., Olszewski-Kubilius, P., & Worrell, F. C. (2011). Rethinking giftedness and gifted education: A proposed direction forward based on psychological science. *Psychological*

Science in the Public Interest, 12, 3–54. doi:10.1177.15291006 11418029.

Tangney, J. P., Baumeister, R. F., & Boone, A. L. (2004). High self-control predicts good adjustment, less pathology, better grades, and interpersonal success. *Journal of Personality, 72,* 271–324.

Texas Education Agency. (2011). *Texas Essential Knowledge and Skills for Social Studies, Subchapter A. Elementary.* Retrieved from http://ritter.tea.state.tx.us/rules/tac/chapter113/ch113a.pdf

Tomlinson, C. A. (2014). *The differentiated classroom: Responding to the needs of all learners* (2nd ed.). Alexandria, VA: Association for Supervision and Curriculum Development.

Tough, P. (2016, May 25). Why grit can't be taught like math. *EdSurge.* Retrieved from https://www.edsurge.com/news/2016-05-25-why-grit-can-t-be-taught-like-math

Tucker, A. (2012). Jack Andraka, the teen prodigy of pancreatic cancer. *Smithsonian.* Retrieved from http://www.smithsonian mag.com/science-nature/jack-andraka-the-teen-prodigy-of-pancreatic-cancer-135925809

Vallerand, R. J., Blanchard, C., Mageau, G. A., Koestner, R., Ratelle, C., Leonard, M., . . . Marsolais, J. (2003). Les passions de l'âme: On obsessive and harmonious passion. *Journal of Personality and Social Psychology, 85,* 756–767. http://dx.doi.org/10.1037/0022-3514.85.4.756

Wiesel, E. (2006). *Night.* New York, NY: Hill and Wang.

Zimmerman, B. J., & Kitsantas, A. (2014). Comparing students' self-discipline and self-regulation measures and their prediction of academic achievement. *Contemporary Educational Psychology, 39,* 145–155.

About the Author

Laila Y. Sanguras is a former middle school teacher. That means she's an expert in managing parent loops, writing accommodations, field trip planning, and navigating the highs and lows of middle school emotions. Plus, she knows some stuff about language arts.

Her interest in grit stemmed from observing her students balk at challenging activities in school, yet excel despite struggling in areas outside of school. She spent many nights making costumes and planning embarrassing ways she would try to reach her students. But then, she had an ah-ha moment. It wasn't her—it was *them*. That sent her on the grit spiral that you have now joined. Welcome. We're nice here.

She received her doctorate in educational psychology from the University of North Texas. It sounds boring, but really it's exciting. A storyteller at heart, she now deeply understands how she can use numbers *and* words to narrate our experiences.

Printed in the United States
by Baker & Taylor Publisher Services